Codes
and
Coding

Third Edition

STEVEN ROMAN

Emeritus Professor
Department of Mathematics
California State University, Fullerton

Codes and Coding
ISBN 1-878015-21-4

Preface

This is one in a series of mathematics modules designed for the general college level student, whose background may include only intermediate level algebra. It can be used, together with other modules, or as a supplement to another text, in courses such as liberal arts mathematics, finite mathematics, or discrete mathematics.

The goal of this module is to show the reader how mathematics plays a key role in the processing of information in our modern society. We focus on two aspects of information processing, namely encoding for accuracy and encoding for efficiency.

Chapter 1 is devoted to encoding for error detection. In Section 1.1, we discuss several commonly used methods for detecting errors, such as the International Standard Book Number (ISBN), the Universal Product Code (Bar Code), and methods used by major banks. One of the most surprising results to come out of this discussion is that most major institutions do not use the best possible method for error detection! In Section 1.2, we discuss how to judge the quality of the various commonly used methods.

Chapter 2 is devoted to a discussion of the remarkable Hamming code for error correction. In Section 2.1, we describe Hamming codes from an elementary point of view. In Section 2.2, we take another look using a more mathematically sophisticated approach. In Section 2.3, we explore the reasons why the approach taken in the previous section works. This section is optional.

Chapter 3 is devoted to encoding for efficiency. We discuss how to measure efficiency in Section 3.1, and how to construct an efficient code (the Huffman code) in Section 3.2.

The chapters in this module are completely independent of one another, which allows for a great deal of flexibility in covering the material. The entire module can be covered in two to four weeks, depending on depth of coverage. Sections 1.2, 2.2 and 2.3 are the most mathematically sophisticated, and may be skipped without loss of continuity.

Answers to the odd numbered exercises are given in the back of the module, and answers to all of the exercises are available to the instructor upon request.

Preface to the Series

This series is designed to provide textbook material for a course in contemporary mathematics for college level students. For one reason or another, large publishers have not responded to the educational concerns of instructors. Through the use of desktop publishing techniques, this series of modules can provide the needed flexibility to adapt to the differing concerns of instructors and motivational needs of students. In particular, by using these modules, instructors can now select topics on a class-by-class basis. We hope that this series will provide both students and instructors with an adaptable learning tool to help increase enthusiasm for mathematics in the classroom.

Acknowledgments

I would like to express my indebtedness to Professor John G. Pierce for making a number of constructive suggestions for improvements in this module. Also, I am indebted to Ms. Donna Dolan and Ms. Joan Sholars for carefully proofreading the module and working all of the exercises.

Changes for this Edition

The changes for this edition of this module are strictly cosmetic. We are now preparing our modules in EXP for Windows, Version 5.0. As a result, the page location of items may have changed, but there is no content change.

Contents

Introduction

Modern society depends very heavily on the ability to send information from one location to another, as well as to store large quantities of information. Our goal in this module is to see how mathematics plays a key role in these endeavors.

In most cases, information that is to be transmitted or stored must first be prepared, or *encoded* in some way, and this process gives rise to two important issues, namely, how to do the encoding *accurately* and how to do it *efficiently*. Before discussing these issues, let us consider a simple example of encoding.

A computer stores information in an area referred to as its *memory*. This can be thought of as a series of "switches," each of which is always in one of two states — either on or off. This idea is pictured in Figure 1.

Figure 1

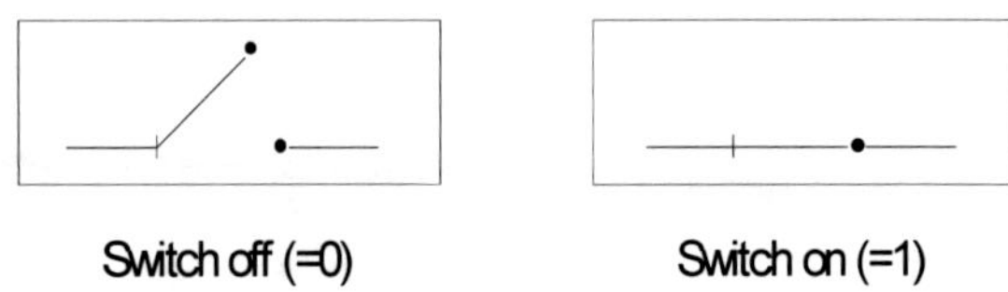

Switch off (=0)   Switch on (=1)

The two states of each switch are usually described by the numbers 0 and 1. Computer scientists use the term **bit** for a 0 or a 1. Thus, each switch stores precisely one bit of information.

A typical computer memory chip, shown here in actual size, can hold up to a million little "switches" of the type shown in Figure 1, that is, a million bits of information.

With this in mind, how shall we store information, such as letters, digits, punctuation marks and other special characters in the memory of a computer?

The answer is that we can *encode* each character as a *string* of 0's and 1's, which can then be stored in several adjacent switches. For instance, if we encode the letter E in the form 01000101, then it can be stored in 8 adjacent switches, as shown in Figure 2. (In order to have enough strings to encode all upper and lower case letters, digits, punctuation marks and other special symbols, we require strings of length at least 8.)

Figure 2

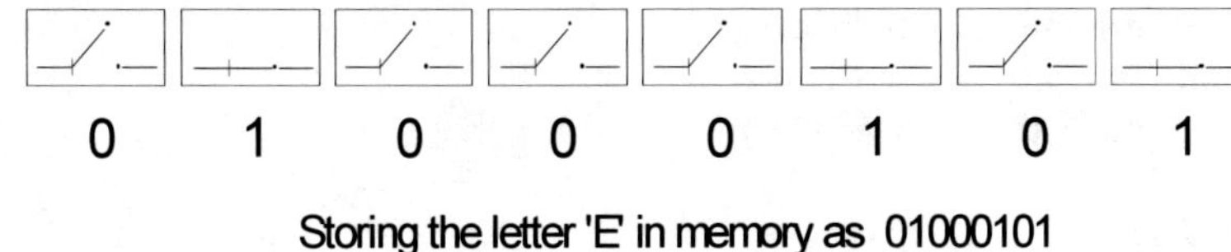

0   1   0   0   0   1   0   1

Storing the letter 'E' in memory as 01000101

The assignment of a string, or codeword, to each commonly used character is referred to as an *encoding scheme*. A portion of the encoding scheme used in the memory of personal computers is shown in Table 1. It is referred to as the ASCII encoding scheme. The acronym ASCII stands for *American Standard Code for Information Interchange*. The complete ASCII encoding scheme is given in the appendix.

Table 1—The ASCII Encoding Scheme		
A → 01000001	J → 01001010	S → 01010011
B → 01000010	K → 01001011	T → 01010100
C → 01000011	L → 01001100	U → 01010101
D → 01000100	M → 01001101	V → 01010110
E → 01000101	N → 01001110	W → 01010111
F → 01000110	O → 01001111	X → 01011000
G → 01000111	P → 01010000	Y → 01011001
H → 01001000	Q → 01010001	Z → 01011010
I → 01001001	R → 01010010	(space) → 00100000

Using the ASCII encoding scheme, we can encode entire messages for storage in the computer.

Example 1

Using Table 1, the message MATH IS FUN is encoded as follows

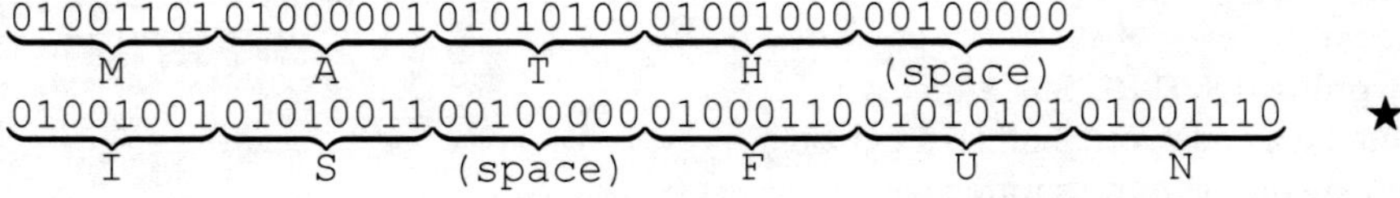

```
01001101 01000001 01010100 01001000 00100000
   M        A        T        H      (space)
01001001 01010011 00100000 01000110 01010101 01001110   ★
   I        S      (space)     F        U        N
```

Encoding for Accuracy

One of the major issues in encoding is that of accuracy. Unfortunately, errors can occur from many different sources. Some errors are due to "natural" causes, such as electrical or magnetic disturbances. Some errors are the result of manufacturing techniques. For instance, storage media such as compact disks have slight irregularities, which can result in errors in stored data. Human beings also introduce errors. For example, mistakes are often made in copying or typing identification numbers, such as driver's license numbers, credit card numbers, or bank account numbers. In Chapters 1 and 2 we will discuss codes that can detect the presence of errors, as well as one code that can actually *correct* some errors!

To illustrate encoding for error detection, let us discuss a simple, yet very widely used method called the *parity check method*. Consider the ASCII code described in Table 1. Suppose that we enlarge each codeword by adjoining either a 0 or a 1 to the *right* end of the word, in such a way that the total number of 1's in the resulting word is even. For instance, since the codeword 01000011 for "C" has an odd number of 1's, we adjoin another 1 on the right, to get 010000111, which has an even number of 1's. On the other hand, since the codeword 01000001 for "A" has an even number of 1's, we adjoin a 0 on the right, to get 010000010, which still has an even number of 1's.

Here are the first three rows of Table 1, with the extra bit adjoined.

A → 010000010	J → 010010101	S → 010100110
B → 010000100	K → 010010110	T → 010101001
C → 010000111	L → 010011001	U → 010101010

As you can see, a 0 is adjoined when the original codeword has an even number of 1's, and a 1 is adjoined when the original codeword has an odd number of 1's. The result is a code in which *every* codeword has an even number of 1's.

The extra bit that we adjoin to make the total number of 1's even is called an **even parity check bit**. (In this context, the word *parity* refers to evenness or oddness.) We could instead adjoin an odd parity check bit to the ASCII code, thus obtaining a code in which every codeword has odd parity. The principle is exactly the same.

Now we come to the purpose of adjoining an even parity check bit. If, in transmitting or storing a codeword, a *single* error is made, the resulting word will have an *odd* number of 1's. For if a 1 is accidentally changed to a 0, then there will be one fewer 1, and if a 0 is accidentally changed into a 1, there will be one more 1. In either case, the number of 1's becomes odd. Hence, simply by counting the number of 1's, we can detect the error!

As an example, suppose we receive the word 010000110. Since this word has an odd number of 1's, we know that it cannot be a codeword, and so an error has been made. Thus, we can request that the codeword be retransmitted.

The parity check method does have its shortcomings. First, when a single error is made, we cannot tell in which position that error occurred, and so we cannot correct that error. Second, the parity check method cannot tell the difference between making 1 error, 3 errors, 5 errors, or indeed any *odd* number of errors. Finally, if any *even* number of errors are made, the parity of the resulting word will still be even, and so an even number of errors cannot be detected at all.

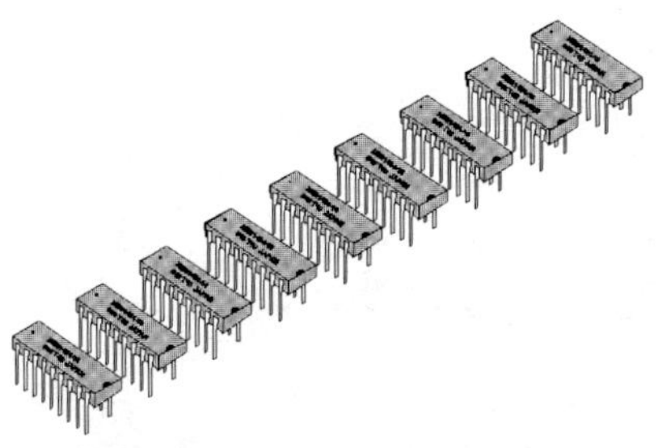

In a typical personal computer, memory chips are aligned in rows of 9 chips. The bits of an 8-bit ASCII codeword are stored in consecutive chips, with the 9-th chip holding the parity check bit. Thus, each row of chips can hold up to a million ASCII codewords, that is, a million characters.

Fortunately, these shortcomings are not really as bad as they might seem. One reason is that, in a reliable system of communication (or storage) the chance of errors occurring is very small, and so when they do occur, it is far more likely that only one error has occurred. Thus, the parity check method will catch "almost" all errors. Also, when the parity check method does detect errors, the codeword in question must generally be retransmitted, and so the issue of exactly how many errors occurred is somewhat irrelevant. Thus, perhaps partly because of the simplicity of the parity check method, it is widely used in the computer industry, and elsewhere. (Parity checking is used in the memory of personal computers, for instance.)

Encoding for Efficiency

Efficiency refers to the ability to send large quantities of information in relatively short periods of time, or to store large quantities of information in a relatively small space. Let us compare the ASCII encoding scheme in Table 1 with the encoding scheme given in Table 2, which is called the **Huffman encoding scheme**, after the mathematician D.A. Huffman, who discovered it in 1952. (The complete Huffman encoding scheme is also given in the appendix.)

Table2-The Huffman Encoding Scheme		
A → 1011	J → 1100001001	S → 0011
B → 100000	K → 11000011	T → 1101
C → 00000	L → 10101	U → 00001
D → 10100	M → 110010	V → 1100000
E → 010	N → 0110	W → 110001
F → 110011	O → 1001	X → 1100001011
G → 100001	P → 100010	Y → 100011
H → 0001	Q → 1100001010	Z → 1100001000
I → 0111	R → 0010	(space) → 111

The Huffman encoding scheme is designed in a very special way so that the more frequently used letters are assigned shorter codewords than less frequently used letters. For instance, the most commonly occurring letter in the English language is "E", and its codeword has the shortest length, whereas "Z" is the least frequently used letter, and its codeword has the longest length. As a result of this design, the *average* codeword length is made as small as possible. Thus, *on the average*, messages will be shorter when encoded with the Huffman encoding scheme rather than the ASCII encoding scheme. Here is an illustration of this.

Example 2

Let us encode the same message as in Example 1, using the Huffman encoding scheme.

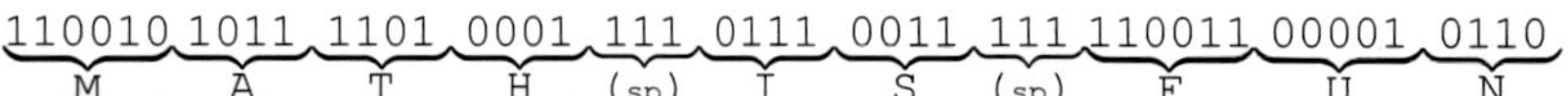

Notice that the Huffman scheme yields an encoded message of length 47 bits, whereas the ASCII encoded message has a length of 88 bits. Thus, the Huffman message is $\frac{47}{88} \approx 53\%$ as large (or 47% shorter) than the ASCII message. (Actually, this comparison is not quite fair, since the ASCII scheme is capable of encoding a lot more messages than the Huffman scheme. Nevertheless, Huffman encoding is more efficient than ASCII encoding.) ★

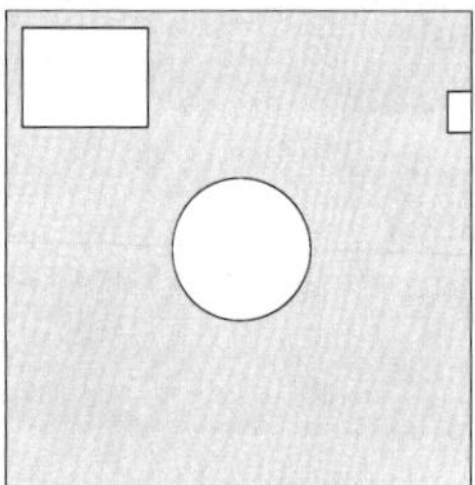

Huffman codes are often used to "pack" data on floppy disks for personal computers.

Not only is the Huffman encoding scheme more efficient than the ASCII scheme, but it is the *most efficient encoding scheme possible*. Our primary goal in Chapter 3 will be to discuss how to construct Huffman encoding schemes.

Let us conclude by setting some terminology that we will use throughout the entire module. If A is a set, then a **word** over A is just a string of elements of A. For instance, if $A = \{0, 1\}$, then

$$0, 001, 101011 \text{ and } 111000111$$

are words over A. In this context, the set A is called an **alphabet**.

A **code** is just a set of words, called **codewords**, over a certain alphabet, called a **code alphabet**. The most commonly used code alphabet is the **binary alphabet** $\{0,1\}$, and a code over the binary alphabet is called a **binary code**. For example, the set

$$C = \{0,01,10,000,1111\}$$

is a binary code, and so is the set of all codewords shown in Table 1. (This is a portion of the **ASCII code**.)

The number of bits in a word is called the **length** of the word. For instance, the binary word $\mathbf{w} = 01101$ has length 5, and the binary words in the ASCII code all have length 8.

A code in which all codewords have the same length is called a **fixed length code**. The ASCII code is an example of a fixed length code. On the other hand, the Huffman code is an example of a **variable length code**, since the codewords have varying lengths.

The set of objects that are to be encoded is referred to as the **source alphabet**. In the case of Table 1, the source alphabet consists of the upper case letters of the Roman alphabet, along with the space character. Finally, an **encoding scheme**, is an assignment of a distinct codeword to each source symbol, as shown in Tables 1 and 2.

EXERCISES

Define or discuss the following terms.

a)	Code	b)	Codeword
c)	Code alphabet	d)	Binary alphabet
e)	Binary code	f)	Bit
g)	Length of a word	h)	Source alphabet
i)	Encoding scheme	j)	Parity
k)	Even parity check bit	l)	Parity check method
m)	Fixed length code	n)	Variable length code

In Exercises 1−12, encode each message using both the ASCII encoding scheme and the Huffman encoding scheme. Then compute how much shorter (or longer) the Huffman message is as compared to the ASCII message, as we did in Example 2.

1.	HALT	2.	HELP ME
3.	I LOVE YOU	4.	SEND CHOCOLATE
5.	TO BE OR NOT TO BE	6.	ROSES ARE RED

7.	VIOLETS ARE BLUE	8.	MOZART IS GREAT
9.	BURGERS AND FRIES	10.	I SHALL RETURN
11.	SEND MONEY FAST	12.	HELP IS ON THE WAY

In Exercises 13—16, decode the given ASCII message.

13. 01010011 01000101 01001110 01000100 00100000
    01001101 01001111 01001110 01000101 01011001

14. 01010011 01000101 01001110 01000100 00100000
    01001101 01001111 01010010 01000101 00100000
    01001101 01001111 01001110 01000101 01011001

15. 01000001 01010100 01010100 01000001 01000011
    01001011 00100000 01000001 01010100 00100000
    01000100 01000001 01010111 01001110

16. 01001000 01000101 01001100 01001100 01001111
    00100000 01000100 01001111 01001100 01001100
    01011001

In Exercises 17—21, decode the given Huffman message.

17. 100001 1001 111 0001 1001 110010 010

18. 110001 1011 0010 111 0111 0011 111
    0001 010 10101 10101

19. 0111 111 1101 0001 0111 0110 11000011
    111 1101 0001 010 0010 010 110011 1001
    0010 010 111 0111 111 1011 110010

(The next two messages have no spaces to separate codewords, but they can still be decoded.)

20. 110001010101011010111110100100010110010

21. 0011100010010101111000011111
    0011100111001111011010101100011

22. Adjoin an even parity check bit to the right end of the given word.

    a) 0001   b) 1110   c) 00000
    d) 110011   e) 1   f) 0

23. Adjoin an odd parity check bit to the right end of the given word.

    a) 0001   b) 1110   c) 00000
    d) 110011   e) 1   f) 0

24. Add an even parity check to every codeword in Table 1.

25. Consider a binary code whose codewords all have length 10. We know from our discussion in the text that if we adjoin an even parity check bit to each codeword, we can detect any odd number of errors in a codeword. Suppose, however, that instead we split each codeword into two 5—bit pieces, and assign an even parity check bit to each piece, as illustrated below

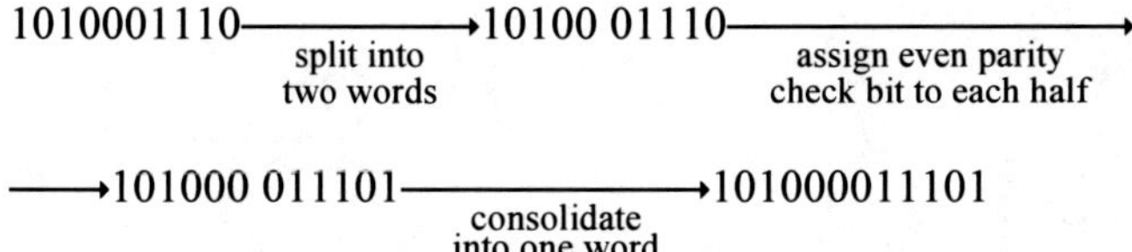

Compare this method to that of adjoining a single parity check bit. Does this method catch more or less errors? Are there any disadvantages to this method?

Chapter 1
Coding for Error Detection

1.1   Check Digit Methods

Let us begin by discussing several simple, yet extremely common, methods for error detection that involve adjoining an extra "digit", called a *check digit*, to the codewords in a code. The simplest example of a *check digit method* is the parity check method that we discussed in the Introduction.

Check digits are used very widely in our society. For instance, airline companies adjoin a check digit to their ticket numbers, banks adjoin a check digit to their bank numbers, the U.S. Post Office, Federal Express and United Parcel Service adjoin a check digit to their invoice numbers, publishing companies adjoin a check digit to their book numbers, many state governments adjoin a check digit to their driver's license numbers, banks adjoin a check digit to major credit card numbers (VISA and Mastercard), and so on. Furthermore, as we will see, some of these methods are significantly better than others at catching errors!

For each example, we will simply indicate how good the method is at catching errors, and save a discussion of the reasons for the next section.

Airline Ticket Numbers

Many airline companies, as well as the United Parcel Service, use a relatively simple check digit method for the detection of errors. Let us illustrate using the airline ticket shown in Figure 1.

Figure 1

FRIENDLY AIRWAYS	PASSANGER TICKET AND BAGGAGE CHECK								
EINSTEIN/A MR									
LOS ANGELES	FA	123	M 27MAY	1730	OK BOWAP 3M			2PC
X LONDON	FA	142	M 28MAY	1415	OK BOWAP 3M			2PC
VIENNA	FA	457	M 03JUN	0755	OK BOWAP 3M			2PC
X LONDON	FA	233	M 03JU N	1200	OK BOWAP 3M			2PC
LOS ANGELES								
USD 1000.00								
XU 13.00				NO CASH REFUND				
USD 1013.00	125 4489643994 3							

The digit immediately following the 10-digit ticket number 4489643994 is a check digit, determined simply by dividing the ticket number by 7, and taking the remainder. In this case, the remainder is 3 so that is the check digit.

Now, suppose that the ticket number (with check digit) is written incorrectly, for instance as 44896539943. Dividing this ticket number by 7 will result in a remainder of 0, which does not match the check digit, and so we know that an error has occurred.

Thus, when a ticket number (with check digit) is input into the airline's computer, the division is performed automatically, and a comparison is made between the remainder and the check digit that was input. If the two numbers do not match, the computer can alert the operator, and request that the ticket number be re−entered.

We should also mention that other institutions, such as the United States postal service, use a similar method on their money orders, but with a divisor of 9 instead of 7.

The Quality of Check Digit Methods

Before looking at other examples of check digit methods, let us consider the question of how to judge the quality of such methods. To judge the quality of a check digit method, we need to know what types of errors are most commonly made when typing or copying large numbers. Various studies have been conducted, and it appears that the most common errors are of three types.

1) **(Format errors)** Omitting a digit (for example, changing 17856 to 1756), or writing a single digit twice (for example, changing 17856 to 178856.)

2) **(Single-digit errors)** Changing a single digit (for example, changing 17856 to 17866.)

3) **(Adjacent transposition errors)** Transposing two adjacent digits (for example, changing 17865 to 18765.)

The first type of error results in a number that has either fewer or more digits than it should have, and so this type of error is easily detected simply by counting the number of digits. Thus, we can measure the quality of a check digit method by how many single-digit or adjacent transposition errors it can detect.

Unfortunately, the airline method misses some errors of both the single-digit and adjacent transposition types, and is in general not a very good method. To illustrate this, consider the following example. If the ticket number 153421 is mistakenly written as 153491 (the 2 has been changed to a 9), then we have

$$\text{incorrect number} = \text{correct number} + 70$$

But, since 70 is divisible by 7, the remainder upon dividing the incorrect number by 7 is the same as the remainder upon dividing the correct number by 7. Hence, the airline method gives the same check digit for the incorrect number as for the correct one, and so it will not catch this particular error.

More generally, the following six single-digit errors will be missed by the airline method

$$0 \to 7, 7 \to 0, 1 \to 8, 8 \to 1, 2 \to 9, 9 \to 2$$

where we have used the notation $0 \to 7$ to mean that a 0 is changed into a 7 in any position in the number, and similarly for the others. The reason that these six errors will be missed is that the result of making any one or more of these errors is a net gain or loss of some multiple of 7, which will not be detected in the remainder when dividing by 7.

Now, the total number of possible single-digit errors is 90. To see this, we note that each such error can be expressed in the form $a \to b$, where a and b are *distinct* digits. But there are 10 possibilities for a (namely, 0,1,2,3,4,5,6,7,8 and 9) and only 9 possibilities for b (since it must be different from a.) This gives a total of $10 \times 9 = 90$ possibilities for $a \to b$, that is, 90 possible single-digit errors.

Thus, the airline method misses 6 out of 90 single-digit errors. Put another way, it catches 84 out of 90 single-digit errors, or $\frac{84}{90} \approx 93\%$ of all single-digit errors. As we will see later in this section, most other commonly used methods catch 100% of all single-digit errors. A similar reasoning can be applied to the adjacent transposition errors, and it can be shown that the airline method catches about 93% of these errors as well.

Universal Product Codes

These days, almost every product found in supermarkets has a bar code printed on its packaging. This code is referred to as a Universal Product Code (UPC), and is designed to be read by optical scanners. However, scanners do make mistakes, and so the UPC has a check digit to help detect errors. Most UPC's are 12-digit codes, such as the one shown in Figure 2, which was taken from a jar of peanut butter. (The scanner reads only the sequence of bars. The printed digits are used in case the UPC must be entered by hand.)

Figure 2

The first digit in the UPC is the symbol code, which is 0 for most products. The next five digits form the company code, and the following five digits form the product code. The last digit is the check digit, which is determined from the first 11 digits. Let us illustrate the procedure with the UPC in Figure 2.

STEP 1

Alternately place the digits 7,9,7,9,... underneath the first 11 digits of the UPC

$$
\begin{array}{ccccccccccc}
0 & 1 & 5 & 5 & 0 & 0 & 1 & 9 & 6 & 2 & 3 \\
7 & 9 & 7 & 9 & 7 & 9 & 7 & 9 & 7 & 9 & 7
\end{array}
$$

STEP 2

Multiply the numbers in each column, and then add the results

$$
\begin{array}{ccccccccccc}
0 & 1 & 5 & 5 & 0 & 0 & 1 & 9 & 6 & 2 & 3 \\
7 & 9 & 7 & 9 & 7 & 9 & 7 & 9 & 7 & 9 & 7 \\
\hline
\end{array}
$$

$$S = \quad 0 \quad +9 \quad +35 \quad +45 \quad +0 \quad +0 \quad +7 \quad +81 \quad +42 \quad +18 \quad +21 \quad = 258$$

The check digit is the remainder obtained by dividing the sum S by 10. In other words, it is the rightmost digit in S, which in this case is 8.

The UPC check digit method can be expressed algebraically as follows. If the 11 digits of the product code (not including the check digit) are $a_1, a_2, \ldots, a_{11}$, then we form the sum

$$S = 7a_1 + 9a_2 + 7a_3 + 9a_4 + 7a_5 + 9a_6 + 7a_7 + 9a_8 + 7a_9 + 9a_{10} + 7a_{11}$$

The check digit is the remainder obtained by dividing S by 10.

The number 10 is referred to as the **modulus** of the check digit method. The numbers 7,9,7,9,7,9,7,9,7,9,7 that appear as the coefficients in the sum S are called the **weights**, and the sum S is called a **weighted sum** of the digits $a_1, a_2, \ldots, a_{11}$. In fact, to make it easier to see the weights in a weighted sum, it is common to write the sum S in the form

$$S = (7,9,7,9,7,9,7,9,7,9,7) \cdot (a_1, a_2, a_3, a_4, a_5, a_6, a_7, a_8, a_9, a_{10}, a_{11})$$

Also, mathematicians have invented a notation that means "take the remainder upon dividing by n." In particular, we write "$k \bmod n$" to denote the remainder obtained by dividing k by n. (mod is short for *modulo*, and $k \bmod n$ is read "k modulo n" or simply "$k \bmod n$.") Here are some examples.

Example 1
---

1) $5 \bmod 2 = 1$ since the remainder obtained by dividing 5 by 2 is 1.
2) $12 \bmod 9 = 3$ since the remainder obtained by dividing 12 by 9 is 3.
3) $176 \bmod 10 = 6$ since the remainder obtained by dividing 176 by 10 is 6.
4) $8 \bmod 9 = 8$ since the remainder obtained by dividing 8 by 9 is 8.
5) $136 \bmod 11 = 4$ since the remainder obtained by dividing 136 by 11 is 4.★

Using this notation, we can say that the check digit for the UPC is given by the formula

check digit
$$= (7,9,7,9,7,9,7,9,7,9,7) \cdot (a_1, a_2, a_3, a_4, a_5, a_6, a_7, a_8, a_9, a_{10}, a_{11}) \bmod 10$$

As an example of the use of this formula, consider the Universal Product Number 0 44300 10625. To compute the check digit, we have

$$
\begin{aligned}
\text{check digit} \\
&= (7,9,7,9,7,9,7,9,7,9,7) \cdot (0,4,4,3,0,0,1,0,6,2,5) \bmod 10 \\
&= (7 \cdot 0 + 9 \cdot 4 + 7 \cdot 4 + 9 \cdot 3 + 7 \cdot 0 + 9 \cdot 0 \\
&\quad + 7 \cdot 1 + 9 \cdot 0 + 7 \cdot 6 + 9 \cdot 2 + 7 \cdot 5) \bmod 10 \\
&= (0 + 36 + 28 + 27 + 0 + 0 + 7 + 0 + 42 + 18 + 35) \bmod 10 \\
&= 193 \bmod 10 \\
&= 3
\end{aligned}
$$

Hence, the complete UPC number is 0 44300 10625 3.

Now let us consider the quality of the UPC check digit method. It is possible to show that the UPC method catches 100% of all single-digit errors, but only 89% of all adjacent transposition errors. We will discuss why this is so in the next section, where we will also explain why the weights 7 and 9 were chosen for the UPC. In any case, the UPC method does a better job than the airline method on single-digit errors, but not quite as good a job on adjacent transposition errors.

Bank Numbers

Many (but not all) banks adjoin a check digit to the bank number that is located in the lower left−hand corner of the bank's checks. Figure 3 shows a reasonable facsimile of a check, with an actual 9-digit bank number.

Figure 3

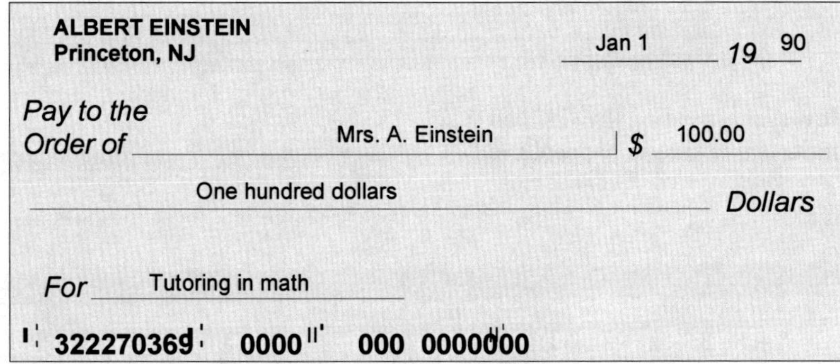

The 9th digit in this number is a check digit, determined by the formula

$$\text{check digit} = (7,3,9,7,3,9,7,3) \cdot (a_1, a_2, a_3, a_4, a_5, a_6, a_7, a_8) \bmod 10$$

This formula is very similar to the one used in the UPC method, but the weights are 7, 3 and 9.

For example, the check digit in Figure 3 is determined as follows.

$$
\begin{aligned}
\text{check digit}\\
&= (7,3,9,7,3,9,7,3) \cdot (3,2,2,2,7,0,3,6) \bmod 10\\
&= (7 \cdot 3 + 3 \cdot 2 + 9 \cdot 2 + 7 \cdot 2 + 3 \cdot 7 + 9 \cdot 0 + 7 \cdot 3 + 3 \cdot 6) \bmod 10\\
&= (21 + 6 + 18 + 14 + 21 + 0 + 21 + 18) \bmod 10\\
&= 119 \bmod 10\\
&= 9
\end{aligned}
$$

Not surprisingly, the bank number method is just as good as the UPC method, that is, it catches 100% of all single-digit errors, and 89% of all adjacent transposition errors. As with the UPC method, we will have more to say about this in the next section.

International Standard Book Numbers

If you look on the back cover (or on the copyright page) of any of your textbooks, you will see a 10-digit number such as

$$0\text{-}15\text{-}541730\text{-}4$$

This is called the *International Standard Book Number*, or ISBN, of the book. The first digit in the ISBN gives the language of the publishing company (0 and 1 are for English, 2 is for French, 3 for German, and so on.) The next group of digits (2 in this case) forms the publisher's code. The next group of digits (6 in this case) forms the publisher's code for that particular book, and the last digit is the check digit.

Check digits for ISBN are determined by the formula

check digit
$$= (1, 2, 3, 4, 5, 6, 7, 8, 9) \cdot (a_1, a_2, a_3, a_4, a_5, a_6, a_7, a_8, a_9) \bmod 11$$

Notice that, in this case the modulus is 11. However, dividing by 11 can produce a remainder of 10, which is not a single digit. If this should happen, the letter X is used for the check digit.

Let us try this formula on the ISBN given above

$$
\begin{aligned}
\text{check digit} \\
&= (1, 2, 3, 4, 5, 6, 7, 8, 9) \cdot (0, 1, 5, 5, 4, 1, 7, 3, 0) \bmod 11 \\
&= (1 \cdot 0 + 2 \cdot 1 + 3 \cdot 5 + 4 \cdot 5 + 5 \cdot 4 + 6 \cdot 1 + 7 \cdot 7 + 8 \cdot 3 + 9 \cdot 0) \bmod 11 \\
&= (0 + 2 + 15 + 20 + 20 + 6 + 49 + 24 + 0) \bmod 11 \\
&= 136 \bmod 11 \\
&= 4
\end{aligned}
$$

The ISBN method turns out to be much better than either the UPC method or the bank method. In fact, the ISBN method catches 100% of all single-digit errors, *and* 100% of all adjacent transposition errors! The price we pay for this accuracy is that we must use a non-digit (namely X) in case the remainder is 10.

The reason that the ISBN method is so good is that the modulus 11 is a *prime* number, that is, it has no divisors other than 1 and itself. We will explore this matter more closely in the next section. In fact, we will show in the next section that *no method using a formula such as the ones used in the UPC and bank number methods, that uses a modulus of 10, can catch 100% of all single-digit errors and 100% of all adjacent transposition errors!* (Do you suppose that the people who invented the ISBN method knew this fact, and that's why they chose modulus 11?)

Despite the results of the previous paragraph, modulus 10 methods remain much more popular than methods using any other modulus. In fact, our next method uses modulus 10, but uses a different method for computing the sum S in such a way as to "squeeze out" every bit of accuracy possible.

Credit Card Numbers

A scheme invented by IBM, and used by credit card companies, libraries and certain foreign banks, differs somewhat from the methods we have discussed so far, and is best described by giving a step-by-step example. Consider the bank number (without check digit)

$$132\ 899\ 572\ 547$$

To determine the check digit, we proceed as follows.

STEP 1
Starting from the right (not the left), alternately place the digits 2,1,2,1,... underneath the digits of the number.

$$\begin{array}{cccccccccccc} 1 & 3 & 2 & 8 & 9 & 9 & 5 & 7 & 2 & 5 & 4 & 7 \\ 1 & 2 & 1 & 2 & 1 & 2 & 1 & 2 & 1 & 2 & 1 & 2 \end{array}$$

STEP 2

Multiply the numbers in each column.

$$\begin{array}{crccccccccccc} & 1 & 3 & 2 & 8 & 9 & 9 & 5 & 7 & 2 & 5 & 4 & 7 \\ \times & 1 & 2 & 1 & 2 & 1 & 2 & 1 & 2 & 1 & 2 & 1 & 2 \\ \hline & 1 & 6 & 2 & 16 & 9 & 18 & 5 & 14 & 2 & 10 & 4 & 14 \end{array}$$

STEP 3

Recopy the numbers in the last row, replacing each two-digit number by the *sum* of the two digits. (For example, replace 16 by $1 + 6 = 7$, and replace 14 by $1 + 4 = 5$.) Don't change the single-digit numbers.

$$\begin{array}{crccccccccccc} & 1 & 3 & 2 & 8 & 9 & 9 & 5 & 7 & 2 & 5 & 4 & 7 \\ \times & 1 & 2 & 1 & 2 & 1 & 2 & 1 & 2 & 1 & 2 & 1 & 2 \\ \hline & 1 & 6 & 2 & 16 & 9 & 18 & 5 & 14 & 2 & 10 & 4 & 14 \\ & 1 & 6 & 2 & 7 & 9 & 9 & 5 & 5 & 2 & 1 & 4 & 5 \end{array}$$

STEP 4

Add the digits in the last row

$$S = 1 + 6 + 2 + 7 + 9 + 9 + 5 + 5 + 2 + 1 + 4 + 5 = 56$$

The check digit is found by multiplying S by 9, and taking the remainder after dividing by 10, that is,

$$\text{check digit} = (9 \cdot S) \bmod 10$$

In this case, since $9 \cdot 56 = 504$, the check digit is 4. Thus, after adjoining the check digit, the number is 132 899 572 547 4.

It is possible to show that the credit card method catches 100% of all single-digit errors, and 98% of all adjacent transposition errors. (The only transposition errors it misses is changing 09 to 90, or vice-versa.) Thus, it is far better than the airline, UPC or bank number method, and almost as good as the ISBN method, but it has the advantage of not requiring the use of a letter as a check digit.

Let us conclude this section by summarizing the various methods.

Method: Airline and United Parcel Service
Formula: check digit = (id number) mod 7
Errors Caught: 93% of all single-digit and 93% of all adjacent transposition

---

Method: Universal Product Code (UPC)
Formula:

check digit
$$= (7, 9, 7, 9, 7, 9, 7, 9, 7, 9, 7) \cdot (a_1, a_2, a_3, a_4, a_5, a_6, a_7, a_8, a_9, a_{10}, a_{11}) \bmod 10$$

Errors Caught: 100% of all single-digit and 89% of all adjacent transposition

---

Method: Bank number
Formula:

$$\text{check digit} = (7,3,9,7,3,9,7,3) \cdot (a_1, a_2, a_3, a_4, a_5, a_6, a_7, a_8) \bmod 10$$

Errors Caught: 100% of all single-digit and 89% of all adjacent transposition

---

Method: International Standard Book Number (ISBN)
Formula:

$$\text{check digit} = (1,2,3,4,5,6,7,8,9) \cdot (a_1, a_2, a_3, a_4, a_5, a_6, a_7, a_8, a_9) \bmod 11$$

Errors Caught: 100% of all single-digit and 100% of all adjacent transposition

---

Method: Credit card
Formula: check digit $= 9 \cdot S \bmod 10$, where S is determined as in the example above
Errors Caught: 100% of all single-digit and 98% of all adjacent transposition

---

EXERCISES

Define or discuss the following terms.

a) Check digit method
b) Check digit
c) Airline method
d) Universal Product Code
e) UPC method
f) Bank number method
g) ISBN
h) ISBN method
i) Credit card method
j) k mod n
k) Weighted sum

In Exercises 1—15, find the correct check digit for the given number using the airline method.

1. 327
2. 202
3. 378
4. 6814
5. 8560
6. 3442
7. 23218
8. 46917
9. 22541
10. 723981
11. 495413
12. 6620600
13. 6326367
14. 884533184
15. 953350528

In Exercises 16—27, find the correct check digit for the given Universal Product Code.

16. 49430041824
17. 87766785215
18. 88950020762
19. 77267915458
20. 11121291030
21. 81204024812
22. 05188056728
23. 72221559420
24. 93975272639
25. 35434464978
26. 17221812058
27. 07625934951

In Exercises 28—39, find the correct check digit for the given bank number.

28. 71521295
29. 84740554
30. 84983267
31. 78247173
32. 43419264
33. 18724997
34. 02716152
35. 64267786
36. 46231498
37. 29157643
38. 75336700
39. 16926964

In Exercises 40—51, find the correct check digit for the given ISBN.

40. 0-59-852922
41. 0-111-39478
42. 2-291-19917
43. 0-486-21694
44. 0-12-043760
45. 3-540-96600
46. 0-7167-8156
47. 0-471-08684
48. 0-15-542736
49. 0-15-571052
50. 0-13-214171
51. 0-13-152447

In Exercises 52—63, find the correct check digit using the credit card method.

52. 0287045
53. 4782001
54. 2003058
55. 98657529
56. 35522836
57. 86122111
58. 912019559
59. 511894727
60. 827495810
61. 7838214962
62. 9518975244
63. 6239377840

64. What percentage of single-digit errors are caught by the method used by the United States postal service? (This method is similar to the Airline method, but uses a divisor equal to 9.)

1.2 Comparing Check Digit Methods

As promised in the previous section, we now turn to a discussion of determining the quality of various check digit methods. The fact that the ISBN method can catch 100% of all single-digit errors and 100% of all adjacent transposition errors raises the question of whether we can do as well with a check digit method that uses modulus 10. Unfortunately, the answer to this question is no. In order to understand this better, we make two definitions.

Definition

An integer greater than 1 is **prime** if it has no divisors other than 1 and itself. ★

    For example, the number 19 is prime, since it has no divisors other than 1 and 19 itself. However, 18 is not prime, since it is divisible by 2. The first few prime numbers are 2, 3, 5, 7, 11,....

Definition

Two positive integers are said to be **relatively prime** if they have no common factors, other than 1. ★

    For example, the integers 9 and 10 are relatively prime, since they have no common factors other than 1. (The factors of 9 are 1, 3 and 9, and the factors of 10 are 1, 2 and 5.) However, the numbers 6 and 9 are not relatively prime, since they are both divisible by 3.

    With the exception of the credit card method, all of the check digit methods that we discussed in the previous section have the form

$$\text{check digit} = (w_1, w_2 \ldots, w_k) \cdot (a_1, a_2, \ldots, a_k) \bmod n \tag{1}$$

where $w_1, w_2, \ldots w_k$ are the weights, $a_1, a_2, \ldots, a_k$ are the digits in the number under consideration, and n is the modulus.

    As it turns out, there is a relationship between the weights w_i and the modulus n that tells us how good the method is at catching single-digit and transposition errors. This is explained in the following theorem.

Theorem 1

Provided that the numbers a_i satisfy $0 \leq a_i < n$, a check digit method that uses formula (1) will catch any single-digit error occurring in the ith position in the number $a_1 a_2 \cdots a_k$ if and only if the ith weight w_i is relatively prime to the modulus n. ★

The condition $0 \leq a_i < n$ simply means that the individual digits in the number in question cannot be larger than the modulus n.

    Let us consider an example of how we might use this theorem.

Example 1

To illustrate Theorem 1, consider the simple check digit formula

$$\text{check digit} = (1, 2, 7) \cdot (a_1, a_2, a_3) \bmod 10$$

In this case, the weights are $w_1 = 1$, $w_2 = 2$ and $w_3 = 7$.

Since the weights $w_1 = 1$ and $w_3 = 7$ are relatively prime to the modulus 10, Theorem 1 tells us that any single-digit error occurring in the first position a_1, or the third position a_3, will be detected by this method. For instance, the single-digit errors $429 \to 129$ and $429 \to 428$ will be caught.

However, since the weight $w_2 = 2$ is not relatively prime to the modulus 10, some (but not necessarily all) errors in the second position will be missed. For instance, the error $729 \to 749$ will be caught, since

$$(1, 2, 7) \cdot (7, 2, 9) \bmod 10 = (7 + 4 + 63) \bmod 10 = 74 \bmod 10 = 4$$

and

$$(1, 2, 7) \cdot (7, 4, 9) \bmod 10 = (7 + 8 + 63) \bmod 10 = 78 \bmod 10 = 8$$

and so the check digits are different. On the other hand, the error $729 \to 779$ will not be caught, since

$$(1, 2, 7) \cdot (7, 2, 9) \bmod 10 = (7 + 4 + 63) \bmod 10 = 74 \bmod 10 = 4$$

and

$$(1, 2, 7) \cdot (7, 7, 9) \bmod 10 = (7 + 14 + 63) \bmod 10 = 84 \bmod 10 = 4$$

and so 729 and 779 have the same check digit. ★

According to Theorem 1, if we want to catch all single-digit errors with a modulus 10 method, we *must* pick all of our weights to be relatively prime to 10. For reasons that we won't go into here, there is no advantage to picking weights that are larger than the modulus, and since 1,3,7 and 9 are the only single-digit numbers relatively prime to 10, we must pick our weights from among these numbers. This explains why the UPC and bank number methods, which use only these weights, do catch all single-digit errors.

Notice also that, since the modulus for the ISBN method is the *prime* number 11, *any* number less than 11 will be relatively prime to 11. This is why the ISBN method can use any weight less than 11, and still catch all single-digit errors.

There is a theorem similar to Theorem 1 concerning transposition errors.

Theorem 2

Provided that $0 \le a_i < n$, a check digit method that uses formula (1) will catch any error resulting from the transposition of the ith and jth positions in the number $a_1 a_2 \cdots a_k$ if and only if the *difference* $w_i - w_j$ of the two corresponding weights is relatively prime to the modulus n. ★

Example 2

As an example of this theorem, let us consider again the check digit formula from the previous example

$$\text{check digit} = (1, 2, 7) \cdot (a_1, a_2, a_3) \bmod 10$$

Suppose we transpose the first and second digits of the number $a_1 a_2 a_3$, that is, we change $a_1 a_2 a_3$ to $a_2 a_1 a_3$. Then since the difference

$$w_2 - w_1 = 2 - 1 = 1$$

is relatively prime to 10, Theorem 2 tells us that such an error will always be caught. However, since the difference

$$w_3 - w_2 = 7 - 2 = 5$$

is not relatively prime to 10, some errors created by transposing the second and third positions will be missed. (Incidentally, in applying Theorem 2, you may subtract the weights in either order.) ★

Recall that the UPC method uses the weights 7 and 9. Unfortunately, the difference $9 - 7 = 2$ is not relatively prime to the modulus 10, and this explains why this method does not catch all adjacent transposition errors. A similar statement holds for the bank number method as well.

In fact, suppose we want to design a modulus 10 check digit method of the form

$$\text{check digit} = (w_1, w_2 \ldots, w_k) \cdot (a_1, a_2, \ldots, a_k) \bmod 10$$

that will catch all single-digit errors *and* all adjacent transposition errors. By Theorem 1, to catch all single-digit errors, we must choose the weights from among the numbers 1,3,7 and 9, since these are the only numbers relatively prime to 10. But according to Theorem 2, to catch all adjacent transposition errors, all of the *differences* between adjacent weights must also be relatively prime to 10.

Unfortunately, however, the difference between any two numbers from among 1,3,7 and 9 is always even, that is, the difference is always divisible by 2, and since 10 is also divisible by 2, *none* of these differences is relatively prime to 10. Hence, we are lead to the conclusion that no such method exists! Let us put this important fact into a theorem.

Theorem 3

There is *no* check digit method using the formula

$$\text{check digit} = (w_1, w_2 \ldots, w_k) \cdot (a_1, a_2, \ldots, a_k) \bmod 10$$

that can catch all single-digit errors *and* all adjacent transposition errors. ★

EXERCISES

Define or discuss each of the following terms.

a) Prime number   b) Relatively prime numbers

1.   Write down the first 10 prime numbers.

In Exercises 2–13, determine whether or not the given numbers are relatively prime.

2.   2 and 4   3.   3 and 8   4.   4 and 9
5.   5 and 25   6.   11 and 2   7.   11 and 11
8.   10 and 30   9.   10 and 15   10. 7 and 210
11. 14 and 15   12. 1 and 4   13. 7 and 77

14. Which positive integers are relatively prime to 1?

15. Consider the following check digit formula

$$\text{check digit} = (2, 3, 9) \cdot (a_1, a_2, a_3) \bmod 10$$

a)   In which positions will single-digit errors always be caught using this formula?
b)   In which positions will transposition errors always be caught?

16. Consider the following check digit formula

$$\text{check digit} = (3, 4, 1) \cdot (a_1, a_2, a_3) \bmod 10$$

a)   In which positions will single-digit errors always be caught using this formula?
b)   In which positions will transposition errors always be caught?

17. Consider the following check digit formula

$$\text{check digit} = (5, 4, 1, 8) \cdot (a_1, a_2, a_3, a_4) \bmod 10$$

a)   In which positions will single-digit errors always be caught using this formula?
b)   In which positions will transposition errors always be caught?

18. Consider the following check digit formula

$$\text{check digit} = (3, 4, 6) \cdot (a_1, a_2, a_3) \bmod 9$$

a)   In which positions will single-digit errors always be caught using this formula?
b)   In which positions will transposition errors always be caught?

19. Consider the following check digit formula

$$\text{check digit} = (1, 5, 7) \cdot (a_1, a_2, a_3) \bmod 8$$

a)   In which positions will single-digit errors always be caught using this formula?
b)   In which positions will transposition errors always be caught?

20. Consider the following check digit formula

$$\text{check digit} = (6, 4, 1, 2) \cdot (a_1, a_2, a_3, a_4) \bmod 7$$

a)   In which positions will single-digit errors always be caught using this formula?

   b)   In which positions will transposition errors always be caught?

21. Consider the following check digit formula

$$\text{check digit} = (7, 4, 9, 2, 8, 5) \cdot (a_1, a_2, a_3, a_4, a_5, a_6) \bmod 13$$

   a)   In which positions will single-digit errors always be caught using this formula?

   b)   In which positions will transposition errors always be caught?

22. If p is a prime number, can you explain why *any* positive integer less than p is relatively prime to p?

Chapter 2
Coding for Error Correction

2.1   Hamming Codes

In the previous chapter, we discussed encoding methods designed to *detect* errors in transmitting, copying or storing information. Now we want to discuss a method that can be used not only to detect errors, but also to *correct* them. The code that we will discuss is one example of a class of codes discovered in 1948 by a computer scientist named Richard Hamming. Hence, these codes are referred to as *Hamming codes*.

It happens that there is one Hamming code for each positive integer $r = 1,2,3,\ldots$. Furthermore, the Hamming code associated with the number r is a fixed length binary code with the property that

> there are a total of $2^{2^r - r - 1}$ codewords in the code, and each codeword has length $2^r - 1$

Thus, for instance, the Hamming code associated with the number $r = 1$ has a total of

$$2^{2^1 - 1 - 1} = 2^0 = 1 \text{ codeword of length } 2^1 - 1 = 1$$

and so it is not very useful. Similarly, the Hamming code associated with the number $r = 2$ has

$$2^{2^2 - 2 - 1} = 2^1 = 2 \text{ codewords of length } 2^2 - 1 = 3$$

and so it is also not very useful. However, the Hamming code associated with the number $r = 3$ has

$$2^{2^3 - 3 - 1} = 2^4 = 16 \text{ codewords of length } 2^3 - 1 = 7$$

and since this is the first useful case, we will study it here.

Incidentally, if you have a calculator, you can verify that the Hamming code for $r = 4$ has

$$2^{2^4-4-1} = 2^{11} = 2048 \text{ codewords of length } 2^4 - 1 = 15$$

and the Hamming code for $r = 5$ has

$$2^{2^5-5-1} = 2^{26} = 67,108,864 \text{ codewords of length } 2^5 - 1 = 31$$

Thus, the Hamming codes get quite large, even for relatively small values of r.

Now, the first step in discussing an encoding scheme is to define the source alphabet. Since we have 16 codewords at our disposal, we are allowed an alphabet of size 16 only, and so we may as well consult the appendix to pick the 16 most commonly used letters in the English language. This will give us the best chance of forming meaningful messages to use as examples (and exercises.) Thus, we take the source alphabet to be

$$\{E,T,A,O,I,N,S,R,H,L,D,U,C,F,M,W\}$$

(Of course, we could have chosen any set of 16 symbols for our source alphabet. Also, if we wanted to use codewords of length 15, then we could have chosen up to 2048 source symbols, which is more than enough for all letters, digits and punctuation marks. Furthermore, a computer could easily handle the added complexity of longer codewords.)

The Hamming encoding scheme for our source alphabet is given in Table 1. (We have listed the letters in alphabetical order, for easier reference. Also, for convenience, another copy of this table appears in the appendix.) Notice that each codeword is a binary word of length 7. Also, while it may not seem so from the table, the codewords are chosen in a very definite way, and we will have more to say about how they are chosen in Section 3.3.

Table 1 - A Hamming Encoding Scheme	
A $\rightarrow$ 0000000	M $\rightarrow$ 1000011
C $\rightarrow$ 0001111	N $\rightarrow$ 1001100
D $\rightarrow$ 0010110	O $\rightarrow$ 1010101
E $\rightarrow$ 0011001	R $\rightarrow$ 1011010
F $\rightarrow$ 0100101	S $\rightarrow$ 1100110
H $\rightarrow$ 0101010	T $\rightarrow$ 1101001
I $\rightarrow$ 0110011	U $\rightarrow$ 1110000
L $\rightarrow$ 0111100	W $\rightarrow$ 1111111

Once the source symbols in our message have been encoded using Table 1, we can transmit them (or store them.) For instance, we would transmit the message "HELLO" in the form

$$\underbrace{0101010}_{H} \quad \underbrace{0011001}_{E} \quad \underbrace{0111100}_{L} \quad \underbrace{0111100}_{L} \quad \underbrace{1010101}_{O}$$

To understand how the Hamming encoding scheme can correct errors, we must first define a special kind of "distance" between binary words. In particular, the **Hamming distance** between two binary words of *the same length* is the number of positions in which the two words differ. For instance, since the words

$$1110 \text{ and } 0111$$

differ in two positions (the first and fourth), the Hamming distance between these two words is 2. It is common to use the letter d for distance, and so we would write

$$d(1110, 0111) = 2$$

Here are some additional examples

$$d(111, 000) = 3, d(11111, 00010) = 4, d(00010, 10011) = 2$$

Notice that the Hamming distance between two words is 0 if and only if the two words are the same in all positions, that is, if and only if the two words are identical.

One very useful interpretation of the Hamming distance between two words is that it is the number of bits that must be changed in one of the words to produce the other word. Put another way, if a certain word $\mathbf{w}_1$ is transmitted, but due to errors the word $\mathbf{w}_2$ is received, then the Hamming distance $d(\mathbf{w}_1, \mathbf{w}_2)$ is just the *number* of errors that occurred in the transmission.

Hamming's method for correcting errors rests on two very special properties that Hamming codes possess. Let us state them in a theorem.

Theorem 1

The following facts are true for the Hamming code given in Table 1.
1) The distance between any two Hamming codewords is *at least* 3.
2) Every binary word of length 7 is either a Hamming codeword, or else it has distance 1 from *exactly one* Hamming codeword.

Proof.
1) Statement 1 can be proved simply by computing the distances between each of the 120 possible pairs of codewords, and observing that they are all at least 3. However, since this is rather lengthy, we will not do so here.
2) First we note that there are a total of $2^7 = 128$ binary words of length 7. (In general, there are 2^n binary words of length n, for any positive integer n. For a proof of this fact, see Theorem 1 of Section 3.2.) Thus, we can prove statement 2 by counting the number of distinct binary words that are either codewords, or have distance 1 from a codeword. If we get a total of 128, this will account for all of the binary words of length 7, and so the statement will be proved.

   Now, we know that there are 16 Hamming codewords. Furthermore, for each codeword $\mathbf{c}$, there are exactly 7 other binary words that have distance 1 from $\mathbf{c}$, since there are exactly 7 ways to change a single bit in $\mathbf{c}$. For instance, if $\mathbf{c} = 0011100$, then we can produce 7 binary words that have distance 1 from $\mathbf{c}$ as shown in Figure 1.

Figure 1

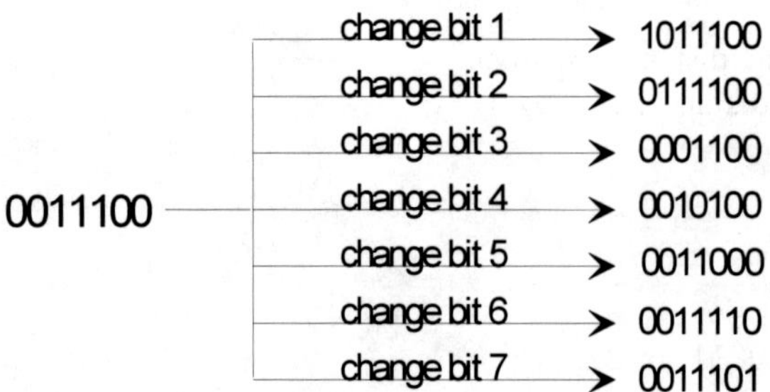

Hence, there are $16 \cdot 7 = 112$ distinct binary words that have distance 1 from a codeword. (We are relying on the fact that, since the distance between codewords is at least 3, no binary word can be a distance 1 from two different codewords.) Finally, if we add to these 112 binary words, the 16 codewords, we get $112 + 16 = 128$, This is what we wanted to show, and statement 2 is proved.★

Now suppose that we are on the receiving end of a transmission. If we receive a word **w** that is a Hamming codeword, we simply decode it using Table 1. But what should we do if errors have occurred, and the received word **w** is not a codeword?

The answer is that we should select the codeword that is "closest" to the received word, using the Hamming distance. According to statement 2 of Theorem 1, there is one and only one codeword **c** that has distance 1 from **w**. For instance, if the received word is **w** = 1100010, then we compute the distance from **w** to each of the 16 Hamming codewords, until we find a codeword that has distance 1 from **w**. This is done in Table 2. (It is easier to compute Hamming distances by writing one word directly below the other.)

Table 2					
0000000	0001111	0010110	0011001	0100101	0101010
1100010	1100010	1100010	1100010	1100010	1100010
$d = 3$	$d = 5$	$d = 4$	$d = 6$	$d = 4$	$d = 2$
0110011	0111100	1000011	1001100	1010101	1011010
1100010	1100010	1100010	1100010	1100010	1100010
$d = 3$	$d = 5$	$d = 2$	$d = 4$	$d = 5$	$d = 3$
1100110					
1100010					
$d = 1$					

This table shows that the received word **w** is closest to the codeword **c** = 1100110, and so we decode **w** as **c**. In other words, we assume that the codeword sent was **c** = 1100110, which is the codeword for the source letter "S".

The method of decoding a received word as the "closest" codeword is called **nearest neighbor decoding**.

The reason for using nearest neighbor decoding becomes apparent when we consider what happens when exactly one error is made in transmitting a codeword **c**. In this case, the received word **w** has distance 1 from **c**, and so nearest neighbor decoding of **w** will select the correct codeword **c**. In other words, in the case of nearest neighbor decoding, a single error is automatically corrected! On the other hand, if two or more errors are made, then the received word **w** will be closer to an incorrect codeword than to the correct codeword, and so nearest neighbor decoding will give us the wrong codeword. Let us summarize these facts in a theorem.

Theorem 2

For a Hamming encoding scheme, if a *single* error occurs in any codeword, then nearest neighbor decoding will correct that error. On the other hand, if more than one error occurs in a codeword, then nearest neighbor decoding will give the wrong codeword. ★

Coding theorists express Theorem 1 by saying that the Hamming encoding scheme is a *single-error-correcting* encoding scheme. In view of Theorem 2, a Hamming encoding scheme is a good choice when the chances of more than one error occurring in the same codeword is remote.

Let us conclude with an example of Hamming decoding.

Example 1

Let us decode the following received message, assuming that at most one error has occurred in any codeword

```
0001111  1010101  0010111  0011001  1100110
0000000  1011010  0011001  0100101  1110000  1011100
```

Using Table 1, we begin decoding (In looking up codewords in Table 1, it helps to notice that the codewords in the left column all begin with a 0, whereas the codewords in the right column all begin with a 1.)

$$0001111 \rightarrow C$$
$$1010101 \rightarrow O$$

Now we come to a word that is not a codeword, namely $\mathbf{w} = 0010111$, and so we begin computing the distance from **w** to each codeword, stopping when we find a codeword that has distance 1 from **w**.

0000000	0001111	0010110
0010111	0010111	0010111
$d = 4$	$d = 2$	$d = 1$

Thus, the correct codeword is 0010110, which we decode as "D". (The error was made in the 7th position.) Let us agree to write

$$0010111 \xrightarrow[\text{corr}]{} D$$

to indicate that the *corrected* word is the codeword for "D". Continuing to decode using Table 1 gives

$$0011001 \to E$$
$$1100110 \to S$$
$$0000000 \to A$$
$$1011010 \to R$$
$$0011001 \to E$$
$$0100101 \to F$$
$$1110000 \to U$$

Again we come to a word 1011100 that is not a codeword, and so we begin computing distances

0000000	0001111	0010110	0011001	0100101	0101010
1011100	1011100	1011100	1011100	1011100	1011100
$d = 4$	$d = 4$	$d = 3$	$d = 3$	$d = 5$	$d = 5$
0110011	0111100	1000011	1001100		
1011100	1011100	1011100	1011100		
$d = 6$	$d = 2$	$d = 5$	$d = 1$		

This shows that the correct codeword is 1001100 (the error was made in the third position), which is the codeword for "N", and so we write

$$1011100 \xrightarrow[\text{corr}]{} N$$

Putting the pieces together, we see that an error occurred in two of the codewords of the original message, and that the corrected message is "CODES ARE FUN". ★

EXERCISES

Define or discuss the following terms.
a)   Hamming distance   b)   Nearest neighbor decoding
c)   Single-error-correcting encoding scheme

In Exercises 1−3, encode the given words using the Hamming encoding scheme of Table 1.
1.   MATHEMATICS   2.   CANDLES   3.   DOLL HOUSE

In Exercises 4—9, the given word is a Hamming codeword in which one error has been made. Determine the correct codeword, and the position where the error occurred.

4. 0100000
5. 0010010
6. 0111010
7. 1001101
8. 1001111
9. 1010010
10. 1010110
11. 0001001
12. 0100111

In Exercises 13—24, decode the given message, assuming that it was encoded using the Hamming code of Table 1, and that no more than one error has occurred in any codeword. Also, indicate where any errors may have occurred. (Spaces have been ignored in these messages.) Hint: In looking up codewords in Table 1, it helps to notice that the codewords in the left column all begin with a 0, whereas the codewords in the right column all begin with a 1.

13. 1000011 0000000 1101001 0111010 0110011 1100110
    1100101 1110000 1001100
14. 1000011 0010000 1101001 0101010 0110011 1100110
    0101010 0000000 1011010 0000110
15. 1111111 0011001 0111000 0110100 0010110 1010101
    1001100 0011001
16. 0001111 1010101 1010011 0011001 0101010 1010101
    0000011 0011001
17. 0110011 0100000 1000111 0001010 1010101 1101001
18. 1100011 0000000 1001100 0111010 0000000 1101001
    1101001 0000000 1001000
19. 1101001 0101010 0011001 1110011 0011010 0100110
    0110011 1100110 0101010 0011001 1011010 0011001
20. 0000111 1010101 0010110 0011001 1100110 0000000
    1011010 0011001 1001100 0011001 0000000 1101011
21. 1011010 1100000 1001100 0100101 0000000 1100110
    1101001 0011001 1011010
22. 1000011 0010011 1100110 1100101 1010101 1011010
    1000011 1010101 1101001 0101010 0011001 1011010
23. 0001111 0101010 1110101 0011111 1010101 0111100
    0000000 1101001 0011001 0110011 1100110 1001100
    0110011 0011111 0011001
24. 0110011 1100110 0100010 0000000 0111100 0111100
    1011010 1011001 1101001 1110000 1011010 1001100

2.2   Another Approach to Hamming Codes

In the previous section, we took a very straightforward approach to Hamming codes. First, we described the codewords in a table. For reference, we repeat that table here.

Table 1 - A Hamming Encoding Scheme	
A → 0000000	M → 1000011
C → 0001111	N → 1001100
D → 0010110	O → 1010101
E → 0011001	R → 1011010
F → 0100101	S → 1100110
H → 0101010	T → 1101001
I → 0110011	U → 1110000
L → 0111100	W → 1111111

Then we discussed the fact that every *non*-codeword **w** has distance 1 from exactly one codeword **c**, and so if a non-codeword **w** is received, we should interpret it as being that codeword **c**. This is referred to as *nearest neighbor decoding*.

Thus, when a non-codeword **w** is received, we compute its distance from each codeword, until we come upon the nearest codeword **c**. While this may take several distance computations, the procedure is certainly not hard to carry out. Unfortunately, however, for larger Hamming codes, it can be much too time consuming.

In this section, we will take another look at Hamming codes from a somewhat more sophisticated viewpoint — one that Hamming himself might have used. We will see that some additional mathematics can make the decoding much easier. In fact, we won't need to compute a single distance! In the next section, we will discuss the details of why this approach to Hamming codes actually works, and at the same time, discover how Hamming picked his codewords.

In order to properly understand Hamming's approach, we need to develop several mathematical concepts. Some of these concepts may seem strange to you, but we think that if you bear with it, you will be rewarded by a clearer understanding of the beauty of Hamming codes.

We begin with a look at the binary number system.

The Binary Number System

As you know, the number system that we humans use is the *decimal*, or *base 10* number system, where each digit in a number represents a certain power of 10. For instance,

$$83506 = 8 \times 10^4 + 3 \times 10^3 + 5 \times 10^2 + 0 \times 10^1 + 6 \times 10^0$$

where $10^0 = 1$.

As you can see from our discussion of memory in the Introduction to this module, most machines, including computers, are not very well suited to the decimal number system. However, they are well suited to the *binary*, or *base 2* number system.

In the binary number system, instead of the *digits* 0,1,2,3,4,5,6,7,8 and 9, we use the *bits* 0 and 1. Thus, a binary number is a sequence of 0's and 1's, each of which represents a certain power of 2. For instance,

$$101001 = 1 \times 2^5 + 0 \times 2^4 + 1 \times 2^3 + 0 \times 2^2 + 0 \times 2^1 + 1 \times 2^0$$

where $2^0 = 1$.

In order to avoid confusion when using more than one number system at a time, it is common to use subscripts to distinguish the bases, as in 83506_{10} and 101001_2. Here are some additional examples of converting from binary representation to decimal.

Example 1

To convert the binary number 1110_2 to decimal, we write

$$1110_2 = 1 \times 2^3 + 1 \times 2^2 + 1 \times 2^1 + 0 \times 2^0 = 8 + 4 + 2 + 0 = 14_{10}$$

To convert the binary number 1101001_2 to decimal, we write

$$\begin{aligned}
1101001_2 \\
&= 1 \times 2^6 + 1 \times 2^5 + 0 \times 2^4 + 1 \times 2^3 + 0 \times 2^2 + 0 \times 2^1 + 1 \times 2^0 \\
&= 64 + 32 + 0 + 8 + 0 + 0 + 1 \\
&= 105_{10}
\end{aligned}$$

Since we will not need to convert numbers from decimal representation to binary, we will defer the details of that procedure to the appendix. For our discussion of Hamming codes, however, we will have use for the first few decimal numbers, written as 3-bit binary numbers, as in Table 2.

Table 2	
Decimal	Binary
0	000
1	001
2	010
3	011
4	100
5	101
6	110
7	111

Addition Modulo 2

You are no-doubt familiar with several different number systems, such as the whole number system, the integers, the rational numbers, and so on. Mathematicians often work in other number systems, however, and we will need to do so here. The number system we need is, fortunately, the simplest of all. It is just the set $\{0,1\}$, consisting of the numbers 0 and 1. We multiply these numbers in the usual way, that is,

$$0 \cdot 0 = 0, 0 \cdot 1 = 0, 1 \cdot 0 = 0, 1 \cdot 1 = 1$$

However, we cannot use ordinary addition, since $1+1 = 2$, which is *not* in our number system. Instead, we use an operation referred to as *addition modulo 2*, denoted by the symbol $\oplus$, and defined by

$$0 \oplus 0 = 0, 0 \oplus 1 = 1, 1 \oplus 0 = 1, 1 \oplus 1 = 0$$

Notice that addition modulo 2 is the same as ordinary addition except for the fact that $1 \oplus 1 = 0$. Notice also that the operation $\oplus$ is the same as taking the ordinary sum $+$, then dividing by 2 and keeping only the remainder. In symbols,

$$a \oplus b = (a + b)\,\mathrm{mod}\,2$$

and this is precisely why $\oplus$ is referred to as addition modulo 2.

Although addition modulo 2 may seem a bit peculiar, it has a large number of interesting applications, one of which is to the subject we are now discussing. (Incidentally, to the best of my knowledge, no−one has been able to think of a good way to *read* the expression $a \oplus b$, so you might try "*a* funny plus *b*.")

Since we will often want to add a long string of 0's and 1's together, it is very helpful to observe that the sum will be equal to 0 when there is an even number of 1's, and 1 when there are an odd number of 1's. For instance,

$$0 \oplus 1 \oplus 1 \oplus 1 \oplus 0 \oplus 0 \oplus 1 = 0$$

since there are an even number of 1's on the left side.

Finally, we should mention that mathematicians use the symbol $\mathbb{Z}_2$ (read "zee two") to denote the number system $\{0,1\}$, together with the operations of multiplication, and addition modulo 2.

Matrices of 0's and 1's

Another very useful tool for our discussion is the *matrix*. A **matrix** is just a rectangular array of numbers, such as

$$\begin{bmatrix} 1 & 0 & 0 \end{bmatrix}, \begin{bmatrix} 1 & 1 \\ 0 & 1 \end{bmatrix}, \begin{bmatrix} 1 & 1 & 1 \\ 0 & 1 & 0 \end{bmatrix} \text{ and } \begin{bmatrix} 0 \\ 1 \\ 1 \\ 1 \\ 0 \end{bmatrix}$$

(The plural of matrix is *matrices*.)

Each of the 0's and 1's in these matrices is called an **entry**. In general, entries may be numbers from any number system, but we are interested here only in matrices whose entries are from the number system $\mathbb{Z}_2$. If a matrix has r rows and c columns, we say that it has **size** $r \times c$. For instance, the matrices above have size $1 \times 3, 2 \times 2, 2 \times 3$ and 4×1, respectively.

If a matrix has only one row, we often refer to it as a **row matrix**, and if a matrix has only one column, we refer to it as a **column matrix**. For instance, the first matrix above is a row matrix, and the last one is a column matrix.

Now we want to define a special kind of "multiplication" for matrices. To begin, we define the product of a row and a column.

$$\begin{bmatrix} a_1 & a_2 & \cdots & a_n \end{bmatrix} \begin{bmatrix} b_1 \\ b_2 \\ \vdots \\ b_n \end{bmatrix} = a_1 b_1 \oplus a_2 b_2 \oplus \cdots \oplus a_n b_n$$

This definition tells us in words that, to form the product, we multiply *corresponding* entries in each matrix, and then use addition modulo 2 to add the results. (If you have seen matrix multiplication before, then you probably have seen this equation, but with ordinary plus signs on the right. Recall, however, that we are working here in the number system $\mathbb{Z}_2$, where "addition" is addition modulo 2, denoted by $\oplus$.)

Before doing some examples, we should remark that, in order for this definition to make sense, the row matrix and column matrix must have the same length, that is, the same number of entries.

Example 2

1) $\begin{bmatrix} 1 & 0 \end{bmatrix} \begin{bmatrix} 1 \\ 1 \end{bmatrix} = 1 \cdot 1 \oplus 0 \cdot 1 = 1 \oplus 0 = 1$

2) $\begin{bmatrix} 1 & 0 & 1 \end{bmatrix} \begin{bmatrix} 1 \\ 1 \\ 0 \end{bmatrix} = 1 \cdot 1 \oplus 0 \cdot 1 \oplus 1 \cdot 0 = 1 \oplus 0 \oplus 0 = 1$

3) $\begin{bmatrix} 0 & 1 & 1 & 0 \end{bmatrix} \begin{bmatrix} 0 \\ 1 \\ 1 \\ 0 \end{bmatrix} = 0 \cdot 0 \oplus 1 \cdot 1 \oplus 1 \cdot 1 \oplus 0 \cdot 0 = 0 \oplus 1 \oplus 1 \oplus 0 = 0$

4) $\begin{bmatrix} 1 & 0 & 1 & 1 & 0 & 1 & 0 \end{bmatrix} \begin{bmatrix} 0 \\ 0 \\ 0 \\ 1 \\ 1 \\ 1 \\ 1 \end{bmatrix}$

$\qquad = 1 \cdot 0 \oplus 0 \cdot 0 \oplus 1 \cdot 0 \oplus 1 \cdot 1 \oplus 0 \cdot 1 \oplus 1 \cdot 1 \oplus 0 \cdot 1$
$\qquad = 0 \oplus 0 \oplus 0 \oplus 1 \oplus 0 \oplus 1 \oplus 0$
$\qquad = 0$

$$\bigstar$$

Strictly speaking, we should have placed small brackets around each of the answers in the preceding example, treating the answer as a matrix of size 1×1. For instance, part 1 should have been written

$$[1 \quad 0]\begin{bmatrix} 1 \\ 1 \end{bmatrix} = [1]$$

However, it is customary to think of matrices of size 1×1 simply as numbers, and to drop the bracket notation, and so we will do this here as well.

As the following example shows, even if the first matrix has more than one row, we can still take the product. (However, here we cannot drop the brackets for the final result.)

Example 3

To take the product

$$\begin{bmatrix} 1 & 1 \\ 0 & 1 \end{bmatrix}\begin{bmatrix} 1 \\ 0 \end{bmatrix}$$

we take the product of *each* row on the left with the column matrix on the right, and use the results to form a new column matrix, as follows

$$\begin{bmatrix} 1 & 1 \\ 0 & 1 \end{bmatrix}\begin{bmatrix} 1 \\ 0 \end{bmatrix} = \begin{bmatrix} 1 \cdot 1 \oplus 1 \cdot 0 \\ 0 \cdot 1 \oplus 1 \cdot 0 \end{bmatrix} = \begin{bmatrix} 1 \oplus 0 \\ 0 \oplus 0 \end{bmatrix} = \begin{bmatrix} 1 \\ 0 \end{bmatrix}$$

Here is another example,

$$\begin{bmatrix} 1 & 1 & 0 \\ 0 & 1 & 1 \end{bmatrix}\begin{bmatrix} 1 \\ 0 \\ 1 \end{bmatrix} = \begin{bmatrix} 1 \cdot 1 \oplus 1 \cdot 0 \oplus 0 \cdot 1 \\ 0 \cdot 1 \oplus 1 \cdot 0 \oplus 1 \cdot 1 \end{bmatrix} = \begin{bmatrix} 1 \oplus 0 \oplus 0 \\ 0 \oplus 0 \oplus 1 \end{bmatrix} = \begin{bmatrix} 1 \\ 1 \end{bmatrix}$$

Here is one final example, of the size we will need to describe Hamming's method.

$$\begin{bmatrix} 0 & 0 & 0 & 1 & 1 & 1 & 1 \\ 0 & 1 & 1 & 0 & 0 & 1 & 1 \\ 1 & 0 & 1 & 0 & 1 & 0 & 1 \end{bmatrix}\begin{bmatrix} 1 \\ 0 \\ 1 \\ 1 \\ 0 \\ 1 \\ 0 \end{bmatrix} = \begin{bmatrix} 0 \oplus 0 \oplus 0 \oplus 1 \oplus 0 \oplus 1 \oplus 0 \\ 0 \oplus 0 \oplus 1 \oplus 0 \oplus 0 \oplus 0 \oplus 1 \oplus 0 \\ 1 \oplus 0 \oplus 1 \oplus 0 \oplus 0 \oplus 0 \oplus 0 \end{bmatrix} = \begin{bmatrix} 0 \\ 0 \\ 0 \end{bmatrix}$$

★

Now we have done the hard work, and we can reap the benefits.

Hamming Codes Revisited

Now we are ready to describe Hamming's method for correcting single errors. By way of example, consider the codeword

$$\mathbf{c} = 1101001$$

Suppose we deliberately introduce an error into the *third position* of this codeword, getting

$$\mathbf{u} = 1111001$$

Hamming devised a very simple, and elegant, scheme for determining the position in which the error has occurred which, in this case, is position 3. For his scheme, he uses the following special matrix, which has come to be called the **Hamming matrix**

$$H = \begin{bmatrix} 0 & 0 & 0 & 1 & 1 & 1 & 1 \\ 0 & 1 & 1 & 0 & 0 & 1 & 1 \\ 1 & 0 & 1 & 0 & 1 & 0 & 1 \end{bmatrix}$$

While this matrix may look complicated, it is quite simple if you observe that the first *column* 001 is nothing more than the binary representation of the number 1, the second column 010 is the binary representation of the number 2, and so on. The 7th column 111 is the binary representation of the number 7. This makes the Hamming matrix easy to remember.

Here is Hamming's scheme.

STEP 1:

Write the received word **u** in the form of a column matrix

$$\mathbf{u} = \begin{bmatrix} 1 \\ 1 \\ 1 \\ 1 \\ 1 \\ 0 \\ 0 \\ 1 \end{bmatrix}$$

STEP 2:

Multiply it by the Hamming matrix

$$\begin{bmatrix} 0 & 0 & 0 & 1 & 1 & 1 & 1 \\ 0 & 1 & 1 & 0 & 0 & 1 & 1 \\ 1 & 0 & 1 & 0 & 1 & 0 & 1 \end{bmatrix} \begin{bmatrix} 1 \\ 1 \\ 1 \\ 1 \\ 0 \\ 0 \\ 1 \end{bmatrix} = \begin{bmatrix} 0 \oplus 0 \oplus 0 \oplus 1 \oplus 0 \oplus 0 \oplus 1 \\ 0 \oplus 1 \oplus 1 \oplus 0 \oplus 0 \oplus 0 \oplus 1 \\ 1 \oplus 0 \oplus 1 \oplus 0 \oplus 0 \oplus 0 \oplus 1 \end{bmatrix} = \begin{bmatrix} 0 \\ 1 \\ 1 \end{bmatrix}$$

STEP 3:

Take the resulting column matrix and write it, *from the top down*, as a *binary number*, getting 011. This binary number is the position of the error. In this case, 011 is the binary representation of 3, and so the error occurred in the *third* position of the original codeword, just as we had arranged!

The binary number we obtain in this fashion is called the **syndrome** of the received word **u**. In the previous example, the syndrome was 011. Thus, the syndrome gives the position of the error.

We should also mention that, if the received word **u** is actually a codeword, that is, if no errors have occurred, then the syndrome will be equal to 0. In other words, this method even tells us when no error has occurred!

Let us try another example, without knowing the correct codeword ahead of time.

Example 4

Suppose we receive the word **u** = 1001101. First, we place the word into a column matrix

$$\mathbf{u} = \begin{bmatrix} 1 \\ 0 \\ 0 \\ 1 \\ 1 \\ 0 \\ 1 \end{bmatrix}$$

Then we multiply by the Hamming matrix

$$\begin{bmatrix} 0 & 0 & 0 & 1 & 1 & 1 & 1 \\ 0 & 1 & 1 & 0 & 0 & 1 & 1 \\ 1 & 0 & 1 & 0 & 1 & 0 & 1 \end{bmatrix} \begin{bmatrix} 1 \\ 0 \\ 0 \\ 1 \\ 1 \\ 0 \\ 1 \end{bmatrix} = \begin{bmatrix} 0 \oplus 0 \oplus 0 \oplus 1 \oplus 1 \oplus 0 \oplus 1 \\ 0 \oplus 0 \oplus 0 \oplus 0 \oplus 0 \oplus 0 \oplus 1 \\ 1 \oplus 0 \oplus 0 \oplus 0 \oplus 1 \oplus 0 \oplus 1 \end{bmatrix} = \begin{bmatrix} 1 \\ 1 \\ 1 \end{bmatrix}$$

Hence, the syndrome is 111, which is the binary representation of the decimal number 7. This tells us that the error has occurred in the 7th position of the received word **u** = 1001101. Changing the 7th position of **u** gives the codeword **c** = 1001100, which according to Table 1, is the codeword for "N". ★

While it is true that multiplying matrices takes a bit of getting used to, hopefully, you will agree that Hamming's method is much more elegant than computing distances! In the next section, we will discuss the reasons why Hamming's method works so elegantly.

EXERCISES

Define or discuss the following concepts.

a)   Decimal number system   b)   Binary number system
c)   Addition modulo 2   c)   Matrix
d)   Entry   e)   The size of a matrix

f)   Row matrix   g)   Column matrix
h)   Hamming matrix   i)   Syndrome

In Exercises 1−12, convert the number from binary to decimal representation.
1.   1   2.   11   3.   101
4.   1101   5.   1000   6.   1011
7.   1111   8.   10010   9.   110110
10. 11111   11. 101111   12. 100000000

In Exercises 13−25, perform the given operations.
13. $5 \oplus 1$ 14. $2 \oplus 2$ 15. $3 \oplus 4$
16. $4 \oplus 3$ 17. $6 \oplus 9$ 18. $12 \oplus 5$
19. $17 \oplus 19$ 20. $10 \oplus 1$ 21. $0 \oplus 5$
22. $1 \oplus 1 \oplus 0 \oplus 0 \oplus 1 \oplus 1$
23. $1 \oplus 0 \oplus 0 \oplus 1 \oplus 1$
24. $1 \oplus 1 \oplus 1 \oplus 1 \oplus 1 \oplus 1 \oplus 1 \oplus 1$
25. $1 \oplus 1 \oplus 1 \oplus 1 \oplus 1 \oplus 1 \oplus 1 \oplus 1 \oplus 1 \oplus 1$

In Exercises 26− 39, take the matrix product.

26. $\begin{bmatrix} 1 & 1 \end{bmatrix} \begin{bmatrix} 1 \\ 1 \end{bmatrix}$

27. $\begin{bmatrix} 0 & 0 \end{bmatrix} \begin{bmatrix} 1 \\ 1 \end{bmatrix}$

28. $\begin{bmatrix} 1 & 1 & 1 \end{bmatrix} \begin{bmatrix} 1 \\ 0 \\ 1 \end{bmatrix}$

29. $\begin{bmatrix} 1 & 0 & 0 \end{bmatrix} \begin{bmatrix} 1 \\ 0 \\ 0 \end{bmatrix}$

30. $\begin{bmatrix} 1 & 0 & 1 & 0 \end{bmatrix} \begin{bmatrix} 1 \\ 1 \\ 0 \\ 0 \end{bmatrix}$

31. $\begin{bmatrix} 1 & 0 & 1 & 0 & 1 \end{bmatrix} \begin{bmatrix} 0 \\ 1 \\ 0 \\ 1 \\ 0 \end{bmatrix}$

32. $\begin{bmatrix} 1 & 1 \\ 1 & 1 \end{bmatrix} \begin{bmatrix} 1 \\ 1 \end{bmatrix}$

33. $\begin{bmatrix} 1 & 0 \\ 0 & 1 \end{bmatrix} \begin{bmatrix} 1 \\ 1 \end{bmatrix}$

34. $\begin{bmatrix} 0 & 0 \\ 0 & 0 \end{bmatrix} \begin{bmatrix} 1 \\ 1 \end{bmatrix}$

35. $\begin{bmatrix} 1 & 1 & 1 \\ 0 & 0 & 0 \end{bmatrix} \begin{bmatrix} 1 \\ 1 \\ 1 \end{bmatrix}$

36. $\begin{bmatrix} 1 & 0 & 1 \\ 0 & 1 & 0 \end{bmatrix} \begin{bmatrix} 0 \\ 1 \\ 0 \end{bmatrix}$

37. $\begin{bmatrix} 1 & 1 & 0 & 0 \\ 0 & 0 & 1 & 1 \\ 1 & 1 & 0 & 0 \end{bmatrix} \begin{bmatrix} 1 \\ 1 \\ 1 \\ 0 \end{bmatrix}$

38. $\begin{bmatrix} 1 & 1 & 1 & 1 \\ 0 & 0 & 0 & 0 \\ 1 & 0 & 1 & 0 \end{bmatrix} \begin{bmatrix} 1 \\ 1 \\ 1 \\ 1 \end{bmatrix}$

39. $\begin{bmatrix} 1 & 0 & 0 & 0 \\ 0 & 1 & 0 & 0 \\ 0 & 0 & 1 & 0 \\ 0 & 0 & 0 & 1 \end{bmatrix} \begin{bmatrix} 1 \\ 0 \\ 1 \\ 0 \end{bmatrix}$

In Exercises 40−45, multiply the given matrix by the Hamming matrix H.

40. $\begin{bmatrix} 0 \\ 1 \\ 0 \\ 0 \\ 1 \\ 0 \\ 1 \end{bmatrix}$ 41. $\begin{bmatrix} 1 \\ 0 \\ 1 \\ 1 \\ 0 \\ 1 \\ 0 \end{bmatrix}$ 42. $\begin{bmatrix} 0 \\ 0 \\ 1 \\ 1 \\ 0 \\ 0 \\ 0 \end{bmatrix}$

43. $\begin{bmatrix} 1 \\ 1 \\ 0 \\ 1 \\ 1 \\ 0 \\ 0 \end{bmatrix}$ 44. $\begin{bmatrix} 1 \\ 1 \\ 0 \\ 1 \\ 1 \\ 1 \\ 1 \end{bmatrix}$ 45. $\begin{bmatrix} 0 \\ 0 \\ 0 \\ 0 \\ 0 \\ 1 \\ 1 \end{bmatrix}$

In Exercises 46–57, a Hamming codeword is given, with one error in it. Determine the correct codeword using the syndrome method, and indicate where the error has occurred.

46. 1101111   47. 1111001   48. 1101011
49. 1011110   50. 1001111   51. 0010011
52. 0010001   53. 0000110   54. 1000010
55. 1000110   56. 1100010   57. 1111000
58. What do you get when you multiply a Hamming codeword by the Hamming matrix?

2.3 Why Hamming Codes Work

By now you are probably wondering where Hamming got his matrix, and why Hamming's syndrome method works. To answer these questions, we need to discuss two additional matters related to matrices.

First, we can extend the operation $\oplus$ defined in the previous section for 0's and 1's, to matrices of 0's and 1's, simply by operating on corresponding entries. For example,

$$\begin{bmatrix} 1 \\ 1 \\ 0 \\ 0 \end{bmatrix} \oplus \begin{bmatrix} 1 \\ 0 \\ 1 \\ 0 \end{bmatrix} = \begin{bmatrix} 1 \oplus 1 \\ 1 \oplus 0 \\ 0 \oplus 1 \\ 0 \oplus 0 \end{bmatrix} = \begin{bmatrix} 0 \\ 1 \\ 1 \\ 0 \end{bmatrix}$$

Notice that this type of "addition" only makes sense if the two matrices have exactly the same size.

Second, the following column matrices will play a special role in our discussion

$$\mathbf{e}_1 = \begin{bmatrix} 1 \\ 0 \\ 0 \\ 0 \\ 0 \\ 0 \\ 0 \end{bmatrix}, \mathbf{e}_2 = \begin{bmatrix} 0 \\ 1 \\ 0 \\ 0 \\ 0 \\ 0 \\ 0 \end{bmatrix}, \dots, \mathbf{e}_7 = \begin{bmatrix} 0 \\ 0 \\ 0 \\ 0 \\ 0 \\ 0 \\ 1 \end{bmatrix}$$

Notice that $\mathbf{e}_1$ has a 1 in the first position, and 0's elsewhere; $\mathbf{e}_2$ has a 1 in the second position, and 0's elsewhere, and so on. In general, $\mathbf{e}_i$ has a 1 in the ith position and 0's elsewhere.

These matrices have a very interesting effect when multiplied by another matrix. For example, if we let

$$A = \begin{bmatrix} 0 & 0 & 0 & 1 & 1 & 1 & 1 \\ 0 & 1 & 1 & 0 & 0 & 1 & 1 \\ 1 & 0 & 1 & 0 & 1 & 0 & 1 \end{bmatrix}$$

then the product $A\mathbf{e}_1$ is

$$\begin{bmatrix} 0 & 0 & 0 & 1 & 1 & 1 & 1 \\ 0 & 1 & 1 & 0 & 0 & 1 & 1 \\ 1 & 0 & 1 & 0 & 1 & 0 & 1 \end{bmatrix} \begin{bmatrix} 1 \\ 0 \\ 0 \\ 0 \\ 0 \\ 0 \\ 0 \end{bmatrix} = \begin{bmatrix} 0 \oplus 0 \oplus 0 \oplus 0 \oplus 0 \oplus 0 \oplus 0 \\ 0 \oplus 0 \oplus 0 \oplus 0 \oplus 0 \oplus 0 \oplus 0 \\ 1 \oplus 0 \oplus 0 \oplus 0 \oplus 0 \oplus 0 \oplus 0 \end{bmatrix} = \begin{bmatrix} 0 \\ 0 \\ 1 \end{bmatrix}$$

Thus, $A\mathbf{e}_1$ is just the first column of A. In general, we have the following useful fact.

Theorem 1

If A is any matrix, then the product $A\mathbf{e}_i$ is just the ith column of A. ★

Now we are ready to turn our attention to understanding Hamming's method. Let's start from scratch, and see if we can't reason it out for ourselves, just as Hamming might have done. Our goal then is to find a matrix — call it A for now — with the property that the syndrome $A\mathbf{u}$ is the binary representation of the position where the error occurred. Ultimately, our reasoning will lead us to the Hamming matrix H, and it will also tell us where Hamming got his codewords, listed in Table 1 of the previous section.

We begin by observing that, if $\mathbf{u}$ is actually a codeword, that is, if no errors have occurred, then we want the syndrome $A\mathbf{u}$ to be the binary representation of the number 0. In other words, we want

$$
A\mathbf{c} = \begin{bmatrix} 0 \\ 0 \\ 0 \end{bmatrix} \text{ for all } \textit{codewords } \mathbf{c}
\tag{1}
$$

Now, to guide our intuition, let us consider an example. Assume that the codeword $\mathbf{c} = 0101010$ was sent, but that an error occurred in the 3−rd position, and we received the word $\mathbf{u} = 0111010$. Writing these words in column matrix notation gives

$$
\mathbf{u} = \begin{bmatrix} 0 \\ 1 \\ 1 \\ 1 \\ 0 \\ 1 \\ 0 \end{bmatrix} \text{ and } \mathbf{c} = \begin{bmatrix} 0 \\ 1 \\ 0 \\ 1 \\ 0 \\ 1 \\ 0 \end{bmatrix}
$$

Of course, these matrices differ only in their 3-rd positions, since that is where the error has occurred. Now, the key point here is that the relationship between $\mathbf{u}$ and $\mathbf{c}$ can be described algebraically by the *matrix equation*

$$
\begin{bmatrix} 0 \\ 1 \\ 1 \\ 1 \\ 0 \\ 1 \\ 0 \end{bmatrix} = \begin{bmatrix} 0 \\ 1 \\ 0 \\ 1 \\ 0 \\ 1 \\ 0 \end{bmatrix} \oplus \begin{bmatrix} 0 \\ 0 \\ 1 \\ 0 \\ 0 \\ 0 \\ 0 \end{bmatrix}
\tag{2}
$$

where the matrix on the far right has 0's in all positions *except* the position where the error has occurred. Equation (2) can be written in the more compact form

$$\mathbf{u} = \mathbf{c} \oplus \mathbf{e}_3 \tag{3}$$

In some sense, the matrix $\mathbf{e}_3$ is a *matrix representation* of the error, and equation (3) can be interpreted by saying that the received word $\mathbf{u}$ is equal to the actual codeword $\mathbf{c}$ "plus" the *error* $\mathbf{e}_3$. Of course, a similar equation holds for errors in any of the other positions.

Now, suppose we multiply equation (3) by a matrix A. This gives

$$A\mathbf{u} = A(\mathbf{c} \oplus \mathbf{e}_3) = A\mathbf{c} \oplus A\mathbf{e}_3$$

or

$$A\mathbf{u} = A\mathbf{c} \oplus A\mathbf{e}_3 \tag{4}$$

Recalling Theorem 1, we know that $A\mathbf{e}_3$ is just the 3-rd column of A. Also, recalling equation (1), we know that $A\mathbf{c}$ is the matrix with all 0 entries. Hence, we can write equation (4) in the form

$$A\mathbf{u} = \begin{bmatrix} 0 \\ 0 \\ 0 \end{bmatrix} \oplus (\text{3-rd column of } A)$$

But adding a matrix all of whose entries are 0's has no effect, and so we get

$$A\mathbf{u} = \text{3-rd column of } A$$

Recall that our goal is to choose A so that $A\mathbf{u}$ is the binary representation of the number 3, since that is the position of the error in this case. Since the binary representation of 3 is 011, we want

$$\begin{bmatrix} 0 \\ 1 \\ 1 \end{bmatrix} = (\text{3-rd column of } A) \tag{5}$$

But this tells us exactly what the 3-rd column of A should be, namely, it should be the binary representation of the number 3!

Similarly, the first column of A should be the binary representation for 1, the second column of A should be the binary representation for 2, and so on. Hence, referring to Table 2 of the previous section, we see that A should be the matrix

$$A = \begin{bmatrix} 0 & 0 & 0 & 1 & 1 & 1 & 1 \\ 0 & 1 & 1 & 0 & 0 & 1 & 1 \\ 1 & 0 & 1 & 0 & 1 & 0 & 1 \end{bmatrix}$$

and this is exactly Hamming's matrix.

In summary, beginning with the goal of wanting the syndrome to tell us the error position, we were able to arrive at equations (1) and (5). Of course, an equation similar to (5) holds for other error positions, and so we actually arrived at the following conclusions.

Conclusion 1:

The ith column of the matrix A must be the binary representation of the number i.

Conclusion 2:

$$A\mathbf{c} = \begin{bmatrix} 0 \\ 0 \\ 0 \end{bmatrix} \text{ for all } codewords\ \mathbf{c}$$

Conclusion 1 tells us that the matrix A must be the Hamming matrix H, and conclusion 2 tells us how to pick the codewords for the Hamming code. In particular, Hamming chose his codewords to be all binary words of length 7 that satisfy the condition

$$H\mathbf{c} = \begin{bmatrix} 0 \\ 0 \\ 0 \end{bmatrix}$$

EXERCISES

In Exercises 1−6, perform the indicated operation.

1. $\begin{bmatrix} 1 \\ 1 \end{bmatrix} \oplus \begin{bmatrix} 1 \\ 0 \end{bmatrix}$ 2. $\begin{bmatrix} 0 \\ 1 \end{bmatrix} \oplus \begin{bmatrix} 1 \\ 0 \end{bmatrix}$ 3. $\begin{bmatrix} 1 \\ 0 \\ 0 \end{bmatrix} \oplus \begin{bmatrix} 0 \\ 1 \\ 0 \end{bmatrix}$

4. $\begin{bmatrix} 1 \\ 1 \\ 1 \end{bmatrix} \oplus \begin{bmatrix} 1 \\ 0 \\ 1 \end{bmatrix}$ 5. $\begin{bmatrix} 1 \\ 0 \\ 0 \\ 0 \end{bmatrix} \oplus \begin{bmatrix} 1 \\ 1 \\ 0 \\ 0 \end{bmatrix}$ 6. $\begin{bmatrix} 1 \\ 0 \\ 1 \\ 1 \end{bmatrix} \oplus \begin{bmatrix} 0 \\ 1 \\ 1 \\ 0 \end{bmatrix}$

In Exercises 7−12, determine the result of multiplying the given matrix by the Hamming matrix, and then do the multiplication to justify your guess.

7. $\mathbf{e}_2$ 8. $\mathbf{e}_3$ 9. $\mathbf{e}_4$

10. $\mathbf{e}_5$ 11. $\mathbf{e}_6$ 12. $\mathbf{e}_7$

Chapter 3
Coding for Efficiency

3.1   Variable Length Codes

Now we are ready to begin a discussion of encoding for efficiency. The ASCII code shown in Table 1 of the Introduction (and in the appendix) has the property that each of its codewords has the same length. This type of code is referred to as a **fixed length code**, and an encoding scheme that uses a fixed length code is called a **fixed length encoding scheme**. On the other hand, the Huffman code in Table 2 of the Introduction (and in the appendix) has the property that its codewords have varying lengths. This type of code is called a **variable length code**, and an encoding scheme that uses such a code is called a **variable length encoding scheme**.

Generally speaking, variable length encoding schemes are more efficient than fixed length schemes, since with a variable length code, we can assign shorter codewords to more frequently occurring source symbols. However, as we will see, variable length encoding schemes do have some disadvantages.

Unique Decipherability

One of the most serious problems that a variable length encoding scheme may have is that it may not be *uniquely decipherable*. By that, we mean that a string of codewords may correspond to more than one message. The following simple example will illustrate this phenomenon.

Example 1

Consider the source alphabet {A,E,R,T}, and the variable length encoding scheme

$$\textbf{Scheme 1}: A \to 00, E \to 1, \ R \to 0, \ T \to 01$$

Suppose we receive the encoded "message" 0001. Unfortunately, this message can be decoded in more than one way, as either "AT", or "ARE", or "RRT" and so on. Hence, this code is not uniquely decipherable.

On the other hand, fixed length codes are always uniquely decipherable. For instance, consider the encoding scheme

$$\textbf{Scheme 2:} A \rightarrow 00, E \rightarrow 01, R \rightarrow 10, T \rightarrow 11$$

This is a fixed length encoding scheme, and we know that every two−bit word must be a codeword. Thus, there is never any problem decoding a message. For example, the message 0011 can only be decoded as "AT", and the message 001001 can only be decoded as "ARE". ★

Let us make the following formal definition.

Definition

An encoding scheme is **uniquely decipherable** if every string of codewords represents *at most one* message.★

Let us emphasize that, to show that an encoding scheme is uniquely decipherable, we must show that *every* string of codewords can represent at most one message. This can be quite difficult to do. However, it is not as hard to show that an encoding scheme is *not* uniquely decipherable, since to do this requires that we find only *one* string of codewords that corresponds to more than one message, as we did in the previous example.

We should also point out that an encoding scheme that is not uniquely decipherable is in general, useless, since we cannot decode messages unambiguously. Hence, when looking for good encoding schemes, we will look only among those that are uniquely decipherable.

Instantaneous Encoding Schemes

When large quantities of information are being communicated, it is often quite difficult, or even impossible, for the person receiving the message to store it before decoding. In such cases, it is essential that the receiver be able to decode the message word-by-word, as it is being received. Let us consider an example.

Example 2

Consider the simple encoding scheme

$$A \rightarrow 0, \ B \rightarrow 00, \ C \rightarrow 000, \ D \rightarrow 0001$$

Suppose we receive the encoded message 00001. Just after the first 0 is received, we cannot tell whether it is the codeword for "A", or the *beginning* of the codeword for "B", "C" or "D". Similarly, after receiving the second 0, we cannot tell whether the two bits 00 represent the codeword for "B" or the beginning of the codeword for "C" or "D". In fact, we cannot begin decoding until the entire message is received. Then we can see that the last 4 bits must be the codeword for "D", and so the message is "AD". ★

When a message can be decoded as it comes in, we can discard the encoded version as soon as it is decoded, and keep only the original message. Hence, we do not have to store the entire encoded message. When an encoding scheme has this property, we call it *instantaneous*.

Definition

An encoding scheme is said to be **instantaneous** if any string of codewords can be decoded as each codeword is received, without having to wait for any additional portion of the message. ★

As an added bonus, an instantaneous encoding scheme is automatically uniquely decipherable.

Theorem 1

An instantaneous encoding scheme is uniquely decipherable.

Proof. If an encoding scheme is instantaneous, then we can decode each codeword as it is received. Hence, no string of codewords could represent two different messages, and so the scheme is uniquely decipherable. ★

As with unique decipherability, it can be difficult to determine directly whether or not an encoding scheme is instantaneous. Fortunately, however, there is a simple way to make this determination, using the concept we discuss next.

The Prefix Property

It is easy to see that the problems we encountered in Example 2 were due to the fact that the codeword for "A" is the same as the *beginning* of the codeword for "B", and similarly for other source letters. Thus, when the codeword for "A" is received, we can't tell whether to decode it as "A", or wait to see if the intended source letter is "B".

This observation leads us to make the following definition. A word **x** is said to be a **prefix** of another word **y** if **y** "begins" with **x**. For instance,

11 is a prefix of 11001
101 is a prefix of 101111
123 is a prefix of 123123
100 is not a prefix of 10111
459 is not a prefix of 45591

Definition

A code C is said to have the **prefix property** if none of the codewords in C are prefixes of any other codeword in C. ★

Determining whether or not a code has the prefix property is simply a matter of checking the codewords, one-by-one, to see if any codeword is the prefix of another. Of course, it helps to order the codewords by increasing length, and take advantage of the fact that no codeword can be a prefix of a *shorter* codeword.

Example 3

The code

$$C = \{0,10,110,1110\}$$

has the prefix property, since

1) 0 is not a prefix of 10, 110 or 1110
2) 10 is not a prefix of 110 or 1110, and
3) 110 is not a prefix of 1110

(1110, being the longest codeword, cannot be a prefix of any other codeword.)
    However, the code

$$\mathcal{D} = \{1,01,00,0001\}$$

does not have the prefix property, since the codeword 00 is a prefix of the codeword 0001. ★

The following theorem gives one reason why codes with the prefix property are so important.

Theorem 2

An encoding scheme is instantaneous if and only if the corresponding code has the prefix property.
Proof. If an encoding scheme is instantaneous, then as soon as a codeword is received, we can decode it. Hence, it cannot be the "beginning", or prefix, of another codeword, and so the code must have the prefix property.
    On the other hand, if a code C has the prefix property, then as soon as a codeword is received, we know that it cannot be the prefix of another codeword, and so we can immediately decode it. Hence, the scheme is instantaneous. ★

Now let us summarize our results.

Theorem 3
---

1) Uniquely decipherable encoding schemes are the only encoding schemes for which messages can be decoded unambiguously. For this reason, we concentrate only on uniquely decipherable encoding schemes.
2) Instantaneous encoding schemes are the only ones with the property that messages can be decoded as the codewords are received. Furthermore, all instantaneous encoding schemes are uniquely decipherable.

3)　An encoding scheme is instantaneous if and only if the corresponding code has the prefix property. ★

As a final step before beginning our search for the most efficient encoding scheme, we must discuss the question of exactly how to measure efficiency in an encoding scheme.

Average Codeword Length

To get an idea how to measure the efficiency of an encoding scheme, consider the following simple example. Suppose we wish to encode the punctuation marks {.,?,!}. Here are two possibilities

Scheme 1:　. $\rightarrow$ 100, ? $\rightarrow$ 11, ! $\rightarrow$ 0
Scheme 2:　. $\rightarrow$ 0, ? $\rightarrow$ 11, ! $\rightarrow$ 100

Even though these two schemes use exactly the same codewords, *with respect to encoding sentences in the English language*, scheme 2 is much more efficient than scheme 1. The reason is that the period occurs much more often in sentences than the exclamation point. Thus, sentences encoded with scheme 2 will tend to be shorter, on the average, than those encoded with scheme 1.

To actually measure the efficiency of these two schemes, we need to know the frequency of occurrence of the three source symbols. Suppose, for instance, that the period occurs about $\frac{4}{5}$ths of the time, and that the question mark and exclamation point each occur about $\frac{1}{10}$ th of the time. Then, *on the average*, we will require

$$\frac{4}{5} \cdot 3 + \frac{1}{10} \cdot 2 + \frac{1}{10} \cdot 1 = \frac{27}{10} = 2.7$$

bits to encode a punctuation mark using scheme 1. (The term $\frac{4}{5} \cdot 3$ comes from the fact that $\frac{4}{5}$th of the time the punctuation mark will be a period, and we will need 3 bits for the codeword. The term $\frac{1}{10} \cdot 2$ comes from the fact that $\frac{1}{10}$th of the time the punctuation mark will be a question mark, and we will need 2 bits for the codeword, and similarly for the last term.)

However, on the average, we require only

$$\frac{4}{5} \cdot 1 + \frac{1}{10} \cdot 2 + \frac{1}{10} \cdot 3 = \frac{13}{10} = 1.3$$

bits to encode a punctuation mark using scheme 2. Hence, scheme 2 is *much* more efficient than scheme 1.

The numbers computed in the previous paragraph are called the *average codeword lengths* of the respective encoding schemes. The average codeword length is a very useful measure of the efficiency of an encoding scheme, but it is important to remember that in order to compute this number, we need to know the relative frequencies of occurrence of each source symbol. Let us make a formal definition of this important concept.

Definition

Let $S = \{s_1, \ldots, s_n\}$ be a source alphabet, and suppose we denote the frequency of occurrence of the letter s_i by *freq*(s_i). Let

$$s_1 \rightarrow c_1, s_2 \rightarrow c_2, \ldots, s_n \rightarrow c_n$$

be an encoding scheme for S, and suppose we denote the length of the codeword c_i by *len*(c_i). Then the **average codeword length** of this encoding scheme is defined to be the number

$$\textit{freq}(s_1) \cdot \textit{len}(c_1) + \textit{freq}(s_2) \cdot \textit{len}(c_2) + \cdots + \textit{freq}(s_n) \cdot \textit{len}(c_n) \qquad \bigstar$$

Example 4

Consider the following encoding scheme, and source letter frequencies,

$$A \rightarrow 10, B \rightarrow 111, C \rightarrow 110, D \rightarrow 0$$

$$\textit{freq}(A) = 0.25, \textit{freq}(B) = 0.125, \textit{freq}(C) = 0.125, \textit{freq}(D) = 0.5$$

The average codeword length of this encoding scheme is

$$\begin{aligned}
\textit{freq}(A) \cdot \textit{len}&(10) + \textit{freq}(B) \cdot \textit{len}(111) \qquad \bigstar\\
&+ \textit{freq}(C) \cdot \textit{len}(110) + \textit{freq}(D) \cdot \textit{len}(0)\\
&= 0.25 \cdot 2 + 0.125 \cdot 3 + 0.125 \cdot 3 + 0.5 \cdot 1\\
&= 1.75
\end{aligned}$$

Given a source alphabet S, with corresponding frequencies of occurrence, there will in general be many different instantaneous encoding schemes for S. The question is, "Can we find an encoding scheme for S that has the *smallest* average codeword length among all instantaneous encoding schemes?" In 1952, D.A. Huffman found a way to do this, and we will describe his method in the next section.

EXERCISES

Define the following terms.
a) Fixed length encoding scheme   b) Variable length encoding scheme
c) Uniquely decipherable   d) Instantaneous
e) Prefix   f) Prefix property
g) Frequency of occurrence   h) Average codeword length

1. Discuss some of the advantages and disadvantages of fixed and variable length encoding schemes.
2. Discuss some of the advantages of the prefix property. Are there any disadvantages?
3. Construct an example of a fixed length binary code other than one given in the text.
4. Construct an example of a variable length binary code other than one given in the text.

*In Exercises 5 − 14, state whether or not the word **x** is a prefix of the word **y**.*

5. $x = 1, y = 1000$ 6. $x = 10, y = 101111$

7. $x = 01, y = 1001$ 8. $x = 000, y = 00$

9. $x = 111, y = 111$ 10. $x = 0110101, y = 0110101010$

11. $x = 8234, y = 82341$ 12. $x = \text{run}, y = \text{running}$

13. $x = \text{the}, y = \text{this}$ 14. $x = x, y = x{+}y$

15.   Do all fixed length encoding schemes have the prefix property?

In Exercises 16−22, determine whether or not the given code has the prefix property.

16.   1,01,011

17.   0,01,001

18.   1,01,001

19.   11,10,01,00

20.   111,10,101,000

21.   1001111,1101,000,111,1010

22.   011,0111,00,001

In Exercises 23−28, compute the average codeword lengths of the two encoding schemes, and determine which scheme is more efficient.

23. $S = \{A,B,C\}$; $freq(A) = 1/6, freq(B) = 1/3, freq(C) = 1/2$.
     Scheme 1: $A \rightarrow 0$, $B \rightarrow 10$, $C \rightarrow 11$
     Scheme 2: $A \rightarrow 01$, $B \rightarrow 1$, $C \rightarrow 00$

24. $S = \{A,B,C\}$; $freq(A) = 0.5, freq(B) = 0.375, freq(C) = 0.125$.
     Scheme 1: $A \rightarrow 0$, $B \rightarrow 10$, $C \rightarrow 11$
     Scheme 2: $A \rightarrow 10$, $B \rightarrow 0$, $C \rightarrow 1$

25. $S = \{A,B,C,D\}$; $freq(A) = 1/2, freq(B) = 1/4, freq(C) = 1/6,$
     $freq(D) = 1/12$.
     Scheme 1: $A \rightarrow 0$, $B \rightarrow 10$, $C \rightarrow 110$, $D \rightarrow 111$
     Scheme 2: $A \rightarrow 01$, $B \rightarrow 1$, $C \rightarrow 00$, $D \rightarrow 110$

26. $S = \{A,B,C,D\}$; $freq(A) = 0.4, freq(B) = 0.3, freq(C) = 0.2,$
     $freq(D) = 0.1$.
     Scheme 1: $A \rightarrow 0$, $B \rightarrow 10$, $C \rightarrow 110$, $D \rightarrow 111$
     Scheme 2: $A \rightarrow 10$, $B \rightarrow 0$, $C \rightarrow 11$, $D \rightarrow 100$

27. $S = \{A,B,C,D,E\}$; $freq(A) = 1/5, freq(B) = 1/5, freq(C) = 3/10,$
     $freq(D) = 1/10, freq(E) = 1/5$.
     Scheme 1: $A \rightarrow 0$, $B \rightarrow 10$, $C \rightarrow 110$, $D \rightarrow 1110$, $E \rightarrow 11110$
     Scheme 2: $A \rightarrow 000$, $B \rightarrow 001$, $C \rightarrow 010$, $D \rightarrow 011$, $E \rightarrow 100$

28. $S = \{A,B,C,D,E,F\}$; $freq(A) = 0.2, freq(B) = 0.2, freq(C) = 0.3,$
     $freq(D) = 0.1, freq(E) = 0.1, freq(F) = 0.1$.
     Scheme 1: $A \rightarrow 0$, $B \rightarrow 10$, $C \rightarrow 110$, $D \rightarrow 1110$, $E \rightarrow 11110$,
     $F \rightarrow 111110$
     Scheme 2: $A \rightarrow 000$, $B \rightarrow 001$, $C \rightarrow 010$, $D \rightarrow 011$, $E \rightarrow 100, F \rightarrow 101$

29.   If an encoding scheme uses a fixed length code whose codewords have length n, what is the *average* codeword length of this scheme?

30. A **comma code** is a code whose codewords have the form

$$1, \, 01, \, 001, \, 0001, \, \ldots, \, \underbrace{00\cdots0}_{n \text{ 0's}}1$$

Thus, each codeword begins with a string of 0's, and ends with a 1. Can you show that all comma codes have the prefix property?

In Exercises 31 and 32, you may use the fact that there are 2^n binary words of length n. For example, there are $2^1 = 2$ binary words of length 1, there are $2^2 = 4$ binary words of length 2, and there are $2^3 = 8$ binary words of length 3.

31. What is the minimum codeword length that can be used to encode the source alphabet $\{a, b, c, d, e\}$ with a *fixed length* encoding scheme?

32. What is the minimum codeword length that can be used to encode the source alphabet $\{a, b, c, d, e, f, g, h, i\}$ with a *fixed length* encoding scheme?

3.2   Huffman Encoding

Now we are ready to describe how to construct Huffman encoding schemes, which are the most efficient (in the sense of having the smallest average codeword length) among all instantaneous encoding schemes. Let us illustrate Huffman's method with an example.

Example 1

Consider the source alphabet and frequencies shown in the following table

Symbol	Frequency
a	0.31
b	0.10
c	0.19
d	0.25
1	0.10
2	0.05

STEP 1
Draw a small circle for each source symbol, and place one symbol inside each circle, arranged in order of increasing frequency. Then label the circle with the symbol's frequency,

0.05 ②   0.10 ①   0.10 ⓑ   0.19 ⓒ   0.25 ⓓ   0.31 ⓐ

STEP 2
Connect the two leftmost circles to a new circle, as shown below. Label the new circle with the *sum* of the frequencies associated to the original circles. Lower this portion of the figure so that the new circle is at the same level as the other circles.

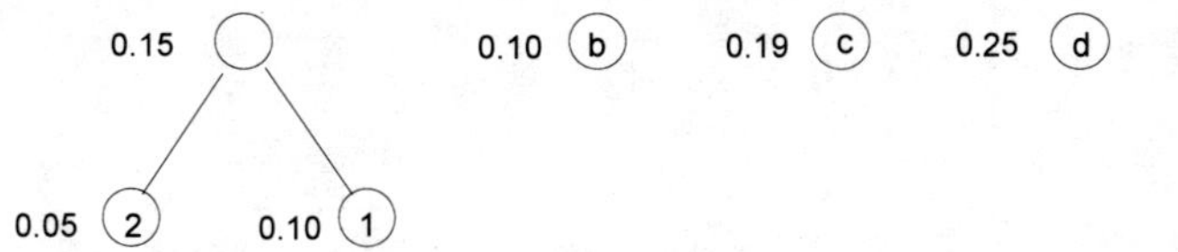

STEP 3
Rearrange the figure so that the circles on the top level are arranged in increasing order of frequencies,

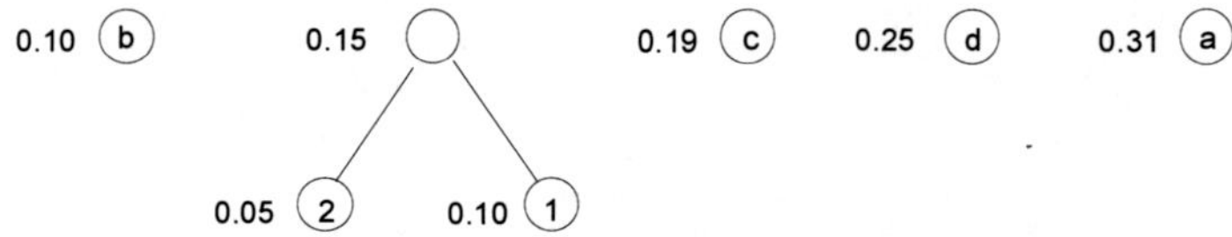

STEP 4
Repeat steps 2 and 3 until the top level of the figure has only one circle

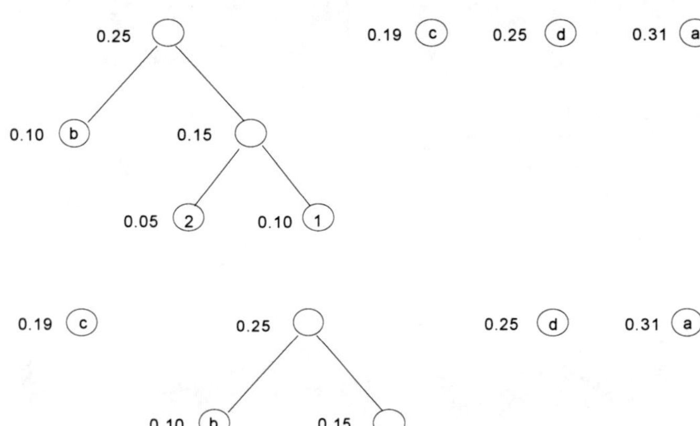

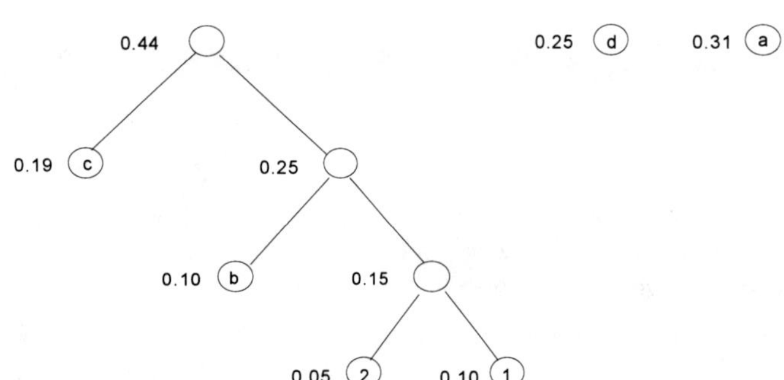

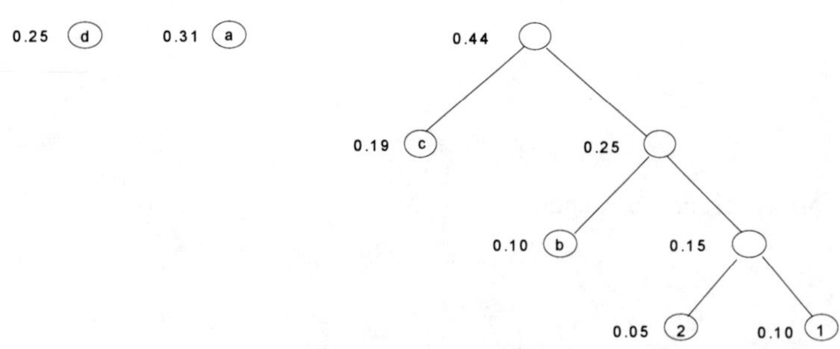

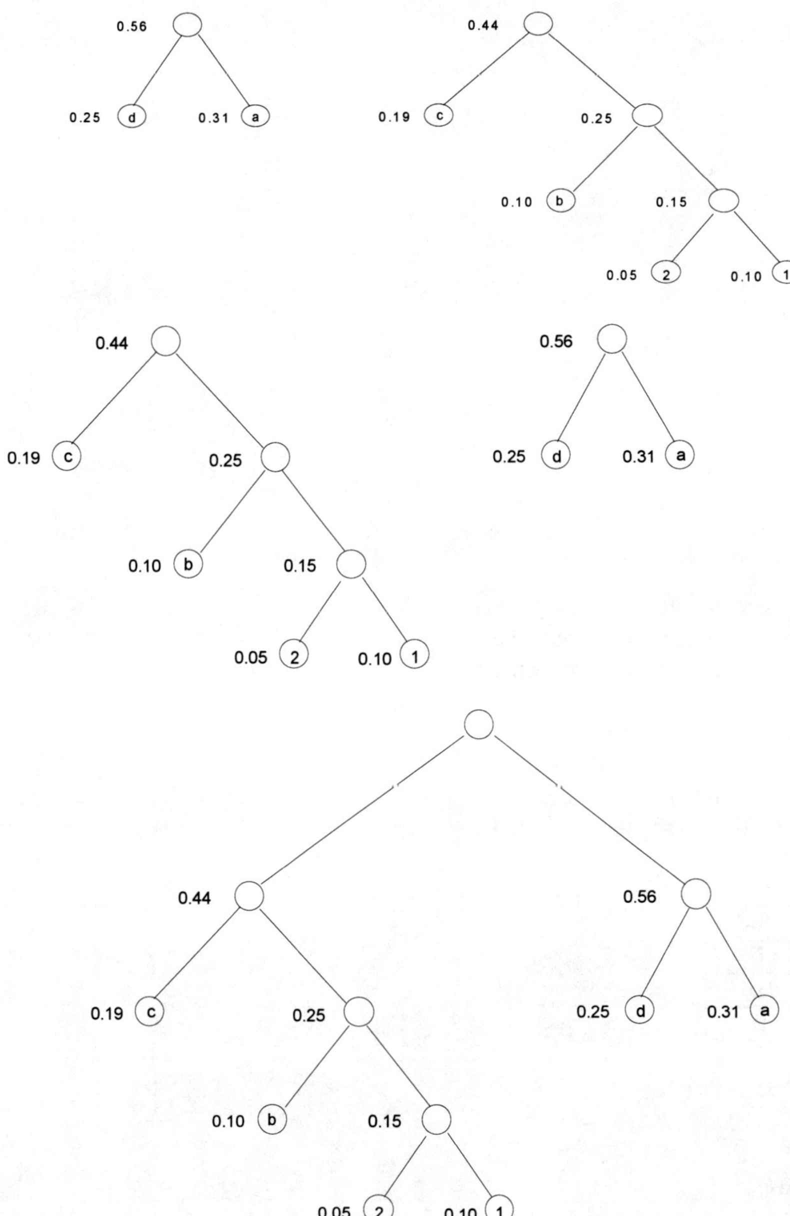

STEP 5

Discard all of the frequencies, and label each line segment that slants up (from left to right) with a 0 and each line segment that slants down (from left to right) with a 1. In this way, we obtain the Huffman tree

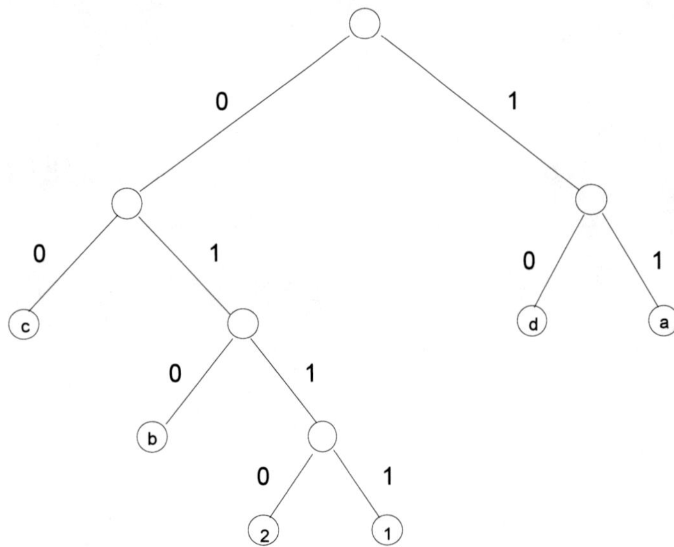

The result is referred to as a **Huffman tree**. The circles are called the **vertices** (singular: **vertex**) or **nodes** of the tree, and the line segments connecting the vertices are called the **edges**. The vertex at the top level is called the **root** of the tree.

In order to obtain the Huffman encoding scheme from the Huffman tree, we start at the top of the tree and follow the edges until we arrive at the source symbol we wish to encode. The sequence of 0's and 1's encountered along the way forms the codeword for that source symbol. In this case, the Huffman encoding scheme is

Source symbol	Frequencies	Code
a	0.31	11
b	0.10	010
c	0.19	00
d	0.25	10
1	0.10	0111
2	0.05	0110

The average codeword length of this encoding scheme is

$$0.31 \cdot 2 + 0.10 \cdot 3 + 0.19 \cdot 2 + 0.25 \cdot 2 + 0.10 \cdot 4 + 0.05 \cdot 4 = 2.40 \qquad \bigstar$$

Example 2

The Huffman encoding scheme given in Table 2 of the Introduction was constructed using the technique described here, with the help of a personal computer. Also with the help of a computer, we computed the average codeword length to be 4.1195. The appendix contains a table showing the frequencies of occurrence for the various letters of the English language, along with a Huffman encoding scheme. ★

In order to get a feel for the savings involved in using a Huffman encoding scheme, we should compare the results of the previous examples with those obtained by using a fixed length encoding scheme. For this, we require the following result.

Theorem 1

There are 2^n binary words of length n.

Proof. To prove this theorem, we simply note that a binary word of length n is formed by filling in each of n positions with a 0 or a 1. Since there are two ways to fill each of the n positions, the total number of ways of forming a binary word of length n is

$$\underbrace{2 \cdot 2 \cdots 2}_{n \text{ factors}} = 2^n \qquad\qquad ★$$

As an example, there are $2^1 = 2$ binary words of length 1, there are $2^2 = 4$ binary words of length 2 (these are 00, 01, 10, 11), and there are $2^3 = 8$ binary words of length 3 (these are 000, 001, 010, 011, 100, 101, 110 , 111).

With the aid of Theorem 1, we can determine how long we must take a fixed length code in order to encode any given source alphabet. For instance, suppose we have a source alphabet consisting of 15 letters. Hence, we need 15 codewords. But since $2^3 = 8$, there are not enough binary words of length 3 to form such a code. On the other hand, since $2^4 = 16$, there are enough codewords of length 4. Thus, to encode a source alphabet of 15 characters, we need a fixed length code of length at least 4.

Now let us look again at Example 1. The source alphabet in that example contains 6 characters. Hence, we require codewords of length at least 3 to form a fixed length encoding scheme for this source. Since for a fixed length scheme, the *average* codeword length is just the common length of the codewords, the average codeword length of such a fixed length encoding scheme is also 3. This compares to the average codeword length of 2.40 for the Huffman encoding scheme. Hence, since

$$\frac{2.40}{3} = 0.80$$

the Huffman scheme is 20% more efficient than a fixed length scheme.

Similarly, the source alphabet in Example 2 has size 27, and so it requires a fixed length code of length at least 5. (Reason: $2^4 = 16 < 27$ but $2^5 = 32 \geq 27$.) Hence, since

$$\frac{4.1195}{5} \approx 0.82$$

we save 18% by using the Huffman encoding scheme.

Finally, we should remark that, given a source S, there may be more than one Huffman encoding scheme for S. That is, Huffman encoding is not unique.

In particular, if different source symbols have the same frequency, the method that we used in the previous examples can lead to different Huffman codes, depending on how we order the source symbols.

EXERCISES

Define or discuss the following terms.
a) Huffman encoding process   b) Huffman tree
c) Vertex   d) Node
e) Edge   f) Root

In Exercises 1−15, construct a Huffman encoding scheme, and compute its average codeword length. Compare this with the average codeword length of a fixed length encoding scheme.

1. $S = \{A,B,C\}$; $freq(A) = 0.4$, $freq(B) = 0.3$, $freq(C) = 0.3$
2. $S = \{A,B,C\}$; $freq(A) = 0.7$, $freq(B) = 0.25$, $freq(C) = 0.05$
3. $S = \{A,B,C,D\}$; $freq(A) = 0.5$, $freq(B) = 0.2$, $freq(C) = 0.2$, $freq(D) = 0.1$
4. $S = \{A,B,C,D\}$; $freq(A) = 0.2$, $freq(B) = 0.1$, $freq(C) = 0.3$, $freq(D) = 0.4$
5. $S = \{A,B,C,D\}$; $freq(A) = 0.25$, $freq(B) = 0.25$, $freq(C) = 0.25$, $freq(D) = 0.25$
6. $S = \{?,!,\#,\$\}$; $freq(?) = 0.9$, $freq(!) = 0.04$, $freq(\#) = 0.01$, $freq(\$) = 0.05$
7. $S = \{A,B,C,D,E\}$; $freq(A) = 0.1$, $freq(B) = 0.2$, $freq(C) = 0.4$, $freq(D) = 0.2$, $freq(E) = 0.1$
8. $S = \{A,B,C,D,E\}$; $freq(A) = 0.1$, $freq(B) = 0.1$, $freq(C) = 0.6$, $freq(D) = 0.1$, $freq(E) = 0.1$
9. $S = \{A,B,C,D,E\}$; $freq(A) = 0.25$, $freq(B) = 0.25$, $freq(C) = 0.25$, $freq(D) = 0.24$, $freq(E) = 0.01$
10. $S = \{1,2,3,4,5\}$; $freq(1) = 0.9$, $freq(2) = 0.05$, $freq(3) = 0.03$, $freq(4) = 0.01$, $freq(5) = 0.01$
11. $S = \{A,B,C,D,E, f\}$; $freq(A) = 0.1$, $freq(B) = 0.2$, $freq(C) = 0.4$, $freq(D) = 0.1$, $freq(E) = 0.1$, $freq(F) = 0.1$
12. $S = \{A,B,C,D,E, f\}$; $freq(A) = 0.9$, $freq(B) = 0.04$, $freq(C) = 0.03$, $freq(D) = 0.01$, $freq(E) = 0.01$, $freq(F) = 0.01$
13. $S = \{A,B,C,D,E, f,G\}$; $freq(A) = 0.1$, $freq(B) = 0.2$, $freq(C) = 0.2$, $freq(D) = 0.1$, $freq(E) = 0.1$, $freq(F) = 0.2$, $freq(G) = 0.1$
14. $S = \{A,B,C,D,E, f,G\}$; $freq(A) = 0.05$, $freq(B) = 0.2$, $freq(C) = 0.35$, $freq(D) = 0.05$, $freq(E) = 0.1$, $freq(F) = 0.2$, $freq(G) = 0.05$
15. $S = \{A,B,C,D,E, f,G\}$; $freq(A) = 0.05$, $freq(B) = 0.1$, $freq(C) = 0.55$, $freq(D) = 0.05$, $freq(E) = 0.1$, $freq(F) = 0.1$, $freq(G) = 0.05$
16. Suppose that you are making up exercises such as Exercises 1−15. What properties do numbers have to possess in order for you to use them as frequencies?

Appendix

The Extended ASCII Code

Char	Binary	Char	Binary	Char	Binary	Char	Binary	Char	Binary
	00000000	4	00110100	g	01100111	Ü	10011010	═	11001101
☺	00000001	5	00110101	h	01101000	¢	10011011	╬	11001110
☻	00000010	6	00110110	i	01101001	£	10011100	╧	11001111
♥	00000011	7	00110111	j	01101010	¥	10011101	╨	11010000
♦	00000100	8	00111000	k	01101011	₧	10011110	╤	11010001
♣	00000101	9	00111001	l	01101100	ƒ	10011111	╥	11010010
♠	00000110	:	00111010	m	01101101	á	10100000	╙	11010011
•	00000111	;	00111011	n	01101110	í	10100001	╘	11010100
◘	00001000	<	00111100	o	01101111	ó	10100010	╒	11010101
○	00001001	=	00111101	p	01110000	ú	10100011	╓	11010110
◙	00001010	>	00111110	q	01110001	ñ	10100100	╫	11010111
♂	00001011	?	00111111	r	01110010	Ñ	10100101	╪	11011000
♀	00001100	@	01000000	s	01110011	ª	10100110	┘	11011001
♪	00001101	A	01000001	t	01110100	º	10100111	┌	11011010
♫	00001110	B	01000010	u	01110101	¿	10101000	█	11011011
☼	00001111	C	01000011	v	01110110	⌐	10101001	▄	11011100
►	00010000	D	01000100	w	01110111	¬	10101010	▌	11011101
◄	00010001	E	01000101	x	01111000	½	10101011	▐	11011110
↕	00010010	F	01000110	y	01111001	¼	10101100	▀	11011111
‼	00010011	G	01000111	z	01111010	¡	10101101	α	11100000
¶	00010100	H	01001000	{	01111011	«	10101110	β	11100001
§	00010101	I	01001001	`|`	01111100	»	10101111	Γ	11100010
▬	00010110	J	01001010	}	01111101	░	10110000	π	11100011
↨	00010111	K	01001011	~	01111110	▒	10110001	Σ	11100100
↑	00011000	L	01001100	⌂	01111111	▓	10110010	σ	11100101
↓	00011001	M	01001101	Ç	10000000	│	10110011	µ	11100110
→	00011010	N	01001110	ü	10000001	┤	10110100	τ	11100111
←	00011011	O	01001111	é	10000010	╡	10110101	Φ	11101000
∟	00011100	P	01010000	â	10000011	╢	10110110	Θ	11101001
↔	00011101	Q	01010001	ä	10000100	╖	10110111	Ω	11101010
▲	00011110	R	01010010	à	10000101	╕	10111000	δ	11101011
▼	00011111	S	01010011	å	10000110	╣	10111001	∞	11101100
	00100000	T	01010100	ç	10000111	║	10111010	φ	11101101
!	00100001	U	01010101	ê	10001000	╗	10111011	ε	11101110
"	00100010	V	01010110	ë	10001001	╝	10111100	∩	11101111
#	00100011	W	01010111	è	10001010	╜	10111101	≡	11110000
$	00100100	X	01011000	ï	10001011	╛	10111110	±	11110001
%	00100101	Y	01011001	î	10001100	┐	10111111	≥	11110010
&	00100110	Z	01011010	ì	10001101	└	11000000	≤	11110011
'	00100111	[	01011011	Ä	10001110	┴	11000001	⌠	11110100
(	00101000	\	01011100	Å	10001111	┬	11000010	⌡	11110101
)	00101001	]	01011101	É	10010000	├	11000011	÷	11110110
*	00101010	^	01011110	æ	10010001	─	11000100	≈	11110111
+	00101011	_	01011111	Æ	10010010	┼	11000101	°	11111000
,	00101100	`	01100000	ô	10010011	╞	11000110	∙	11111001
-	00101101	a	01100001	ö	10010100	╟	11000111	·	11111010
.	00101110	b	01100010	ò	10010101	╚	11001000	√	11111011
/	00101111	c	01100011	û	10010110	╔	11001001	ⁿ	11111100
0	00110000	d	01100100	ù	10010111	╩	11001010	²	11111101
1	00110001	e	01100101	ÿ	10011000	╦	11001011	■	11111110
2	00110010	f	01100110	Ö	10011001	╠	11001100		11111111

THE HUFFMAN CODE

The Huffman Code (Letters listed in order of frequency)		
Symbol	Frequency	Huffman code
(Space)	0.1859	111
E	0.1031	010
T	0.0796	1101
A	0.0642	1011
O	0.0632	1001
I	0.0575	0111
N	0.0574	0110
S	0.0514	0011
R	0.0484	0010
H	0.0467	0001
L	0.0321	10101
D	0.0317	10100
U	0.0228	00001
C	0.0218	00000
F	0.0208	110011
M	0.0198	110010
W	0.0175	110001
Y	0.0164	100011
P	0.0152	100010
G	0.0152	100001
B	0.0127	100000
V	0.0083	1100000
K	0.0049	11000011
X	0.0013	1100001011
Q	0.0008	1100001010
J	0.0008	1100001001
Z	0.0005	1100001000

A Hamming Encoding Scheme	
A → 0000000	M → 1000011
C → 0001111	N → 1001100
D → 0010110	O → 1010101
E → 0011001	R → 1011010
F → 0100101	S → 1100110
H → 0101010	T → 1101001
I → 0110011	U → 1110000
L → 0111100	W → 1111111

The Binary Number System

The following examples will illustrate one method for converting a number from decimal representation to binary representation.

Example 1

To convert the number 13 from decimal to binary, we perform a series of divisions by 2, keeping track of the quotients and the remainders, as follows.

Divisions	Quotients	Remainders
$13 \div 2$	6	1
$6 \div 2$	3	0
$3 \div 2$	1	1
$1 \div 2$	0	1

When the quotient becomes 0, we are done. Now we can write down the desired binary number by reading the remainder column *from the bottom up*, to get 1101_2. In other words, $13_{10} = 1101_2$.

To convert the number 56 from decimal to binary, we write

Divisions	Quotients	Remainders
$56 \div 2$	28	0
$28 \div 2$	14	0
$14 \div 2$	7	0
$7 \div 2$	3	1
$3 \div 2$	1	1
$1 \div 2$	0	1

Reading the remainder column from the bottom up gives $56_{10} = 111000_2$.

To convert the number 147 from decimal to binary, we have

Divisions	Quotients	Remainders
$147 \div 2$	73	1
$73 \div 2$	36	1
$36 \div 2$	18	0
$18 \div 2$	9	0
$9 \div 2$	4	1
$4 \div 2$	2	0
$2 \div 2$	1	0
$1 \div 2$	0	1

Reading the remainder column from the bottom up gives $147_{10} = 10010011_2$. ★

EXERCISES

Convert the following numbers from decimal to binary.

1. 7	2. 10	3. 13
4. 15	5. 21	6. 28
7. 32	8. 45	9. 67
10. 100	11. 125	12. 176
13. 256	14. 300	15. 511

Answers

1. 111	2. 1010	3. 1101
4. 1111	5. 10101	6. 11100
7. 100000	8. 101101	9. 1000011
10. 1100100	11. 1111101	12. 10110000
13. 100000000	14. 100101100	15. 111111111

Answers To Odd Numbered Exercises

Introduction
1. HALT
    ASCII CODE: 01001000 01000001 01001100 01010100
    HUFFMAN CODE: 0001 1011 10101 1101
    53% as long
3. I LOVE YOU
    ASCII CODE: 01001001 00100000 01001100 01001111 01010110
    01000101 00100000 01011001 01001111 01010101
    HUFFMAN CODE: 0111 111 10101 1001 1100000 010 111 100011
    1001 00001
    55% as long
5. TO BE OR NOT TO BE
    ASCII CODE: 01010100 01001111 00100000 01000010 01000101
    0100000 01001111 01010010 00100000 01001110 01001111 01010100
    00100000 01010100 01001111 00100000 01000010 01000101
    HUFFMAN CODE: 1101 1001 111 100000 010 111 1001 0010 111 0110
    1001 1101 111 1101 1001 111 100000 010
    48% as long
7. VIOLETS ARE BLUE
    ASCII CODE: 01010110 01001001 01001111 01001100 01000101
    01010100 01010011 00100000 01000001 01010010 01000101 00100000
    01000010 01001100 01010101 01000101
    HUFFMAN CODE: 1100000 0111 1001 10101 010 1101 0011 111 1011
    0010 010 111 100000 10101 00001 010
    52% as long
9. BURGERS AND FRIES
    ASCII CODE: 01000010 01010101 01010010 01000111 01000101
    01010010 01010011 00100000 01000001 01001110 01000100 00100000
    01000110 01010010 01001001 01000101 01010011
    HUFFMAN CODE: 100000 00001 0010 100001 010 0010 0011 111 1011
    0110 10100 111 110011 0010 0111 010 0011
    53% as long
11. SEND MONEY FAST
    ASCII CODE: 01010011 01000101 01001110 01000100 00100000
    01001101 01001111 01001110 01000101 01011001 00100000 01000110
    01000001 01010011 01010100
    HUFFMAN CODE: 0011 010 0110 10100 111 110010 1001 0110 010
    100011 111 110011 1011 0011 1101
    53% as long
13. SEND MONEY   15. ATTACK AT DAWN
17. GO HOME   19. I THINK THEREFORE I AM
21. SPEAK SOFTLY
23. a) 00010 b) 11100 c) 000001 d) 1100111 e) 10 f) 01

25. This method catches all single errors, as well as all pairs of errors *provided* that the errors occur in different halves of the 10−bit codeword. The price we pay for this is requiring 2 check digits per codeword.

Section 1.1

1.5	3.0	5.6	7.6	9.1	11.2	13.5	15.4	17.6	19.1	21.6
23.3	25.5	27.1	29.1	31.7	33.5	35.2	37.7	39.3	41.3	43.2
45.5	47.3	49.4	51.X	53.4	55.8	57.7	59.3	61.9	63.2	

Section 1.2

1. 2, 3, 5, 7, 11, 13, 17, 19, 23, 29
3. yes   5. no   7. no   9. no   11. yes 13. no
15. a) 2nd, 3rd   b) between 1st and 2nd, 1st and 3rd
17. a) 3rd   b) between 1st and 2nd, 1st and 4th, 2nd and 3rd, 3rd and 4th
19. a) 1st, 2nd and 3rd   b) none
21. a) all positions   b) between all positions

Section 2.1

1. 1000011 0000000 1101001 0101010 0011001 1000011 0000000 1101001 0110011 0001111 1100110
3. 0010110 1010101 0111100 0111100 0101010 1010101 1110000 1100110 0011001
5. D,5   7. N,7   9. R,4   11. E,3
13. MATH IS FUN; H,F 15. WELL DONE; L,L
17. I AM HOT; A,M,H   19. THE IRS IS HERE; I,R,S
21. RUNFASTER;U   23. CHOCOLATEISNICE;O,C,C

Section 2.2

1. 1   3. 5   5. 8   7. 15 9. 54 11. 47 13. 0   15. 1
17. 1   19. 0   21. 1   23. 1   25. 1   27. 0   29. 1   31. 0

33. $\begin{bmatrix} 1 \\ 1 \end{bmatrix}$ 35. $\begin{bmatrix} 1 \\ 0 \end{bmatrix}$ 37. $\begin{bmatrix} 0 \\ 1 \\ 0 \end{bmatrix}$ 39. $\begin{bmatrix} 1 \\ 0 \\ 1 \\ 0 \end{bmatrix}$

41. $\begin{bmatrix} 0 \\ 0 \\ 0 \end{bmatrix}$ 43. $\begin{bmatrix} 0 \\ 1 \\ 0 \end{bmatrix}$ 45. $\begin{bmatrix} 0 \\ 0 \\ 1 \end{bmatrix}$

47. T,3   49. R,5   51. I,2   53. D,3   55. S,2   57. U,4

Section 2.3

1. $\begin{bmatrix} 0 \\ 1 \end{bmatrix}$ 3. $\begin{bmatrix} 1 \\ 1 \\ 0 \end{bmatrix}$ 5. $\begin{bmatrix} 0 \\ 1 \\ 0 \\ 0 \end{bmatrix}$

7. $\begin{bmatrix} 0 \\ 1 \\ 0 \end{bmatrix}$ 9. $\begin{bmatrix} 1 \\ 0 \\ 0 \end{bmatrix}$ 11. $\begin{bmatrix} 1 \\ 1 \\ 0 \end{bmatrix}$

Section 3.1

5. yes   7. no   9. yes   11. yes   13. no

15. Yes, provided that no two codewords are identical.

17. No; 0 is a prefix of 01

19. Yes

21. Yes

23. Scheme 1 length 11/6, scheme 2 length 10/6. Scheme 2 more efficient.

25. Scheme 1 length 21/12, scheme 2 length 22/12. Scheme 1 more efficient.

27. Scheme 1 length 29/10, scheme 2 length 30/10. Scheme 1 more efficient.

29. n   31. 3

Section 3.2

(Recall that Huffman encoding is not unique. Therefore, your answer may differ from ours and still be correct. However, you must get the same average codeword length or else one of us has made a mistake.)

1. $A \to 0, B \to 10, C \to 11$; *len* = 1.6; savings = 20%

3. $A \to 1, B \to 011, C \to 00, D \to 010$; *len* = 1.8; savings = 9%

5. $A \to 10, B \to 11, C \to 00, D \to 01$; *len* = 2; savings = 0%

7. $A \to 1100$, $B \to 10$, $C \to 0$, $D \to 111$, $E \to 1101$;   *len* = 2.2; savings = 27%

9. $A \to 01$, $B \to 00$, $C \to 11$, $D \to 101$, $E \to 100$;   *len* = 2.25; savings = 25%

11. $A \to 1100$, $B \to 10$, $C \to 0$, $D \to 1101$, $E \to 1110$, $F \to 1111$; *len* = 2.4; savings = 20%

13. $A \to 010, B \to 10, C \to 110, D \to 011, E \to 000, F \to 111, G \to 001$; *len* = 2.8; savings = 7%

15. $A \to 01110$, $B \to 000$, $C \to 1$, $D \to 01111$, $E \to 001$, $F \to 010$, $G \to 0110$; *len* = 2.15; savings = 28%